NEGLECTED CUES

Neglected Cues

Kids' Unheard Desires

MARIA M

Spectra Enterprise

Contents

Table of Content

Introduction

Chapter 1: The Symphony of Silence
1.1 Introduction to the concept of overlooked cues in children's behavior.
1.2 Exploring the subtle signals children emit that often go unnoticed.
1.3 Anecdotes and real-life examples illustrating the significance of these cues.

Chapter 2: The Language They Speak
2.1 Delving into the unique communication style of children.
2.2 Unpacking non-verbal cues and expressions that convey unspoken desires.
2.3 How to interpret the language of play, drawings, and gestures.

Chapter 3: The Mask of Normalcy
3.1 Examining the façade of apparent normalcy that conceals deeper needs.
3.2 The impact of societal expectations and parental assumptions on understanding a child's true desires.
3.3 Strategies for peeling back the layers to reveal authentic emotions.

Chapter 4: The Quiet Cravings
4.1 Unveiling the often-overlooked desires that children may not articulate.
4.2 Discussing the difference between expressed wants and unspoken needs.
4.3 Showcasing instances where identifying these desires transformed parent-child dynamics.

Introduction

In the many-sided embroidery of being a parent, where each second winds around a special string in the texture of everyday life, there exists an orchestra of correspondence frequently disregarded — the unobtrusive signs discharged by kids that, as fragile notes in an excellent organization, convey their most profound longings. This book leaves on an excursion to investigate the domain of these dismissed signs, those quiet murmurs lost in the chaos of day to day existence. We dig into the nuanced language of young life, where wants are communicated not just through words however through an intricate transaction of activities, motions, and implicit feelings. It is an investigation of the secret cravings clouded behind the cover of business as usual, the longings that youngsters might battle to well-spoken or that guardians could accidentally excuse. This book looks to unwind the layers of misconception that cover the credible cravings of kids, welcoming perusers to reevaluate their points of view on nurturing and draw in with the significant nuances of their youngster's implicit world.

In the contemporary scene of nurturing, where the speed of life frequently directs the beat, bypassing the peaceful desires of our children is simple. The cutting edge world requests effectiveness and prompt reactions, pretty much ruling out unraveling the multifaceted language of a kid's spirit. However, it is inside these ignored minutes, in the stops among giggling and tears, that the genuine substance of a kid's cravings lies. As we leave on this investigation, it becomes evident that youngsters have a novel and nuanced correspondence style, one that reaches out a long ways past regular verbal articulation. Through play, drawings, and apparently irrelevant signals, they convey a story of wants and feelings that, if inconspicuous, could prompt a significant detach among parent and youngster.

The cover of business as usual, frequently worn by the two kids and guardians the same, disguises a large number of implicit longings. Society forces assumptions on youngsters to adjust to predefined guidelines, and guardians, thusly, may inadvertently form their impression of their kid's necessities in view of cultural standards. This part unfurls the layers of this cultural veneer, encouraging guardians to peer past the surface and draw in with the certified cravings that lie underneath. It prompts an investigation of the effect of cultural and parental presumptions on the comprehension of a kid's actual longings, welcoming reflection on how these suspicions may incidentally ruin the improvement of a more significant parent-kid association.

As we dive into the complexities of these calm desires, it becomes apparent that youngsters may not generally articulate their longings in manners promptly reasonable to grown-ups.

The differentiation between communicated needs and implicit necessities frames a critical part of this investigation. The cravings youngsters harbor are not generally appeared in that frame of mind; all things being equal, they are woven into the texture of their activities and responses. By unraveling these nuanced articulations, guardians can uncover an abundance of knowledge into the internal universe of their kids, encouraging a more significant comprehension of their requirements and goals.

Exploring the close to home territory of life as a youngster is a complicated excursion, set apart by the recurring patterns of a kid's personal scene. This section enlightens the complexities of perceiving and answering profound signals, underlining the essential job feelings play in a youngster's general prosperity. It tends to the difficulties guardians face in unraveling these prompts, giving functional techniques to sustaining the ability to appreciate anyone on a profound level in youngsters. The point is to engage guardians to explore the close to home subtleties of their kid's reality, encouraging a steady climate where feelings are recognized and approved.

Regardless of the all inclusive nature of being a parent, every family is a novel embroidery woven from various strings of culture, custom, and individual encounters. This part examines the potential misinterpretations that can emerge when youngsters' ways of behaving are seen from the perspective of different social and generational points of view. Crossing over the correspondence split among guardians and kids is fundamental for encouraging an association that rises above social contrasts. By understanding the effect of social and generational holes, guardians can explore the sensitive harmony between saving social character and embracing a more adjusted way to deal with nurturing.

In the last sections, the account combines on the subject of association — rediscovering and reviving the connection among parent and kid. It unwinds procedures for revamping and reinforcing this essential relationship, underlining the groundbreaking force of undivided attention and open correspondence. Through a blend of bits of knowledge acquired all through the book, perusers are urged to embrace a more compassionate and adjusted way to deal with nurturing, one that recognizes and answers the unheard cravings of their kids. In doing as such, this investigation serves not just as a manual for translating the unobtrusive signals of experience growing up yet in addition as an encouragement to set out on an excursion toward more resounding and satisfying guardian kid associations.

Chapter 1

The Symphony of Silence

In the fantastic ensemble of presence, there exists a less popular development, a fragile exchange of notes that wind through the texture of our lives — the Orchestra of Quiet. In a world portrayed by the clamor of consistent jabber and the persistent quest for progress, the meaning of quiet frequently slips by everyone's notice. In any case, inside the significant embroidery of quietude lies an orchestra that says a lot, repeating the nuances of the human experience.

Quietness isn't only the shortfall of sound yet a rich and nuanced language of its own, conveying the heaviness of implicit feelings, considerations, and reflections. The Ensemble of Quiet is made out of the stops, the breaths among words, and the snapshots of tranquility that intersperse the hurrying around of our day to day routines. A structure resounds inside the offices of reflection, offering a safe-haven for thought and self-disclosure.

Perhaps of the most strong development inside the Ensemble of Quietness is the quiet of nature. In the calm hug of a peaceful woods or the quieted feel of a serene lake, nature unfurls its quiet ensemble. The stir of leaves, the delicate influence of branches, and the calming cadence of sea waves make an agreeable structure that rises above language.

This quiet exchange with nature has the ability to bring out significant feelings and interface people to an option that could be more significant than themselves — an encounter that words frequently neglect to epitomize.

Inside the domain of human connections, the Orchestra of Quietness takes on an alternate rhythm. There are minutes when words, regardless of how expressive, can't catch the profundity of shared feelings. It is in the common quiet between companions, family, or accomplices that a significant seeing frequently blooms. The implicit signals, the knowing looks, and the tranquil friendship all add to an orchestra that praises the magnificence of association past the limitations of language.

In the isolation of individual reflection, the Ensemble of Quiet turns into a contemplative tune. It is in the quietude of one's own contemplations that the psyche disentangles its intricacies. In the midst of the commotion of the outside world, quietness gives the space to interior exchange, self-revelation, and the development of a more profound comprehension of one's own yearnings, fears, and dreams. This inward ensemble is an individual organization that plays out interestingly for every person, reverberating with the rhythm of their deepest being.

The Ensemble of Quiet additionally tracks down reverberation in the imaginative domains of craftsmanship and articulation. Specialists, authors, and performers frequently draw motivation from the tranquil minutes, utilizing the material of quietness to create their magnum opuses. The pregnant stops in a melodic structure, the clear spaces in a canvas, or the white breadth of a page in writing — all are purposeful decisions that add to the general concordance of imaginative articulation. Without a trace of commotion, inventiveness gets comfortable with its, and the Ensemble of Quiet turns into a dream for the creative soul.

However, in the contemporary scene, the Orchestra of Quietness faces the danger of elimination. The computerized age, with its steady barrage of notices, online entertainment refreshes, and a persevering stream of data, has made a world that fears the quietness of quietness. In this period of availability, veritable snapshots of calm examination have become progressively scant. The specialty of being available in the quiet, of permitting oneself to be encompassed by its tranquility, is continuously getting ceaselessly.

The bedlam of present day life darkens the Ensemble of Quietness as well as decreases the nature of our collaborations. In our current reality where everybody is competing for focus, where the most intense voice frequently rules the discussion, the nuances of quietness are muffled. Certified tuning in, with the expectation to see as opposed to answer, turns into a unique case. The Orchestra of Quiet, when a characteristic piece of the human experience, gambles being eclipsed by the tireless commotion of progress.

Notwithstanding, in the midst of the difficulties, there is trust. The acknowledgment of the worth of quietness is a crucial stage towards recovering the Ensemble of Quiet in our lives. Care practices, reflection, and a cognizant work to make snapshots of calm consideration can act as solutions for the commotion contamination that infests our reality. It is in these deliberate stops that the Ensemble of Quiet recaptures its ability to mend, move, and associate.

The Ensemble of Quietness is an ethereal organization that saturates the actual substance of our reality. A multi-layered ensemble resounds in nature, connections, individual reflection, and imaginative articulation. As we explore the intricacies of the cutting edge world, we actually must perceive and value the significance of quietness in cultivating authentic associations, supporting imagination, and protecting our internal balance. The Ensemble of Quietness welcomes us to check out its unpretentious tunes, empowering an amicable concurrence with the quietude that enhances the human experience.

1.1 Introduction to the concept of overlooked cues in children's behavior.

The mind boggling universe of experience growing up is a domain loaded up with amazement, interest, and vast creative mind. In the midst of the giggling, energy, and the apparently lighthearted nature of kids, there exists an unpretentious and frequently neglected aspect — the domain of disregarded signals in youngsters' way of behaving. These prompts, as unlikely treasures in the embroidered artwork of growing up, convey significant importance, offering bits of knowledge into the implicit cravings, feelings, and necessities of the most youthful citizenry.

Youth, portrayed by quick turn of events and consistent investigation, is a period when youngsters are figuring out how to explore the intricacies of their general surroundings. In their excursion of self-disclosure, they impart through words as well as through a rich embroidery of ways of behaving, articulations, and activities. It is inside these subtleties that the neglected signals arise, shaping a quiet language that, whenever interpreted, gives a more profound comprehension of a kid's inward world.

The idea of ignored prompts in kids' way of behaving envelops many unpretentious signs that might evade relaxed perception. These signs are much of the time communicated through non-verbal communication, changes in disposition, changes in play examples, or even the nuanced tone of a kid's voice. Not at all like express verbal correspondence, these signs work underneath the surface, requiring a sharp eye and a nuanced understanding to unwind the narratives they tell.

One vital part of ignored signals lies in the domain of nonverbal correspondence. Kids, particularly in their early stages, may not have the jargon or the mental capacity to verbally verbalize their considerations and sentiments.

Thusly, their feelings track down appearance through nonverbal means, like looks, motions, and stance. A wrinkled temple, a reluctant grin, or an unexpected change in stance can pass on an abundance of data about a youngster's close to home state, offering a door into their inward world.

Besides, the elements of play act as a prolific ground for the sign of ignored prompts. Play, past its obvious triviality, is a youngster's regular language, a medium through which they investigate, try, and impart. In the realm of play, neglected signs might surface as deviations from typical play designs, inclinations for specific exercises, or the consideration/rejection of explicit components in their creative situations. By diving into the complexities of a drop in the bucket, guardians, teachers, and guardians can acquire significant bits of knowledge into the kid's longings, fears, and developing identity.

Changes in conduct, one more feature of disregarded prompts, can be characteristic of more profound close to home flows. Youngsters, similar to grown-ups, are impacted by different factors like relational intricacies, social cooperations, and natural changes. Unique withdrawal, abrupt explosions of temper, or changes in rest examples might be appearances of fundamental close to home expresses that request consideration. Perceiving these changes in conduct and digging into their main drivers is pivotal for offering the fundamental help and direction to youngsters as they explore the intricacies of their profound scenes.

Besides, the idea of disregarded signals reaches out past individual ways of behaving to include the elements of friend connections and social connections. Kids, in their socialization cycle, are continually finding out about coordinated effort, compassion, and the complexities of shaping associations. The unpretentious signs implanted in their communications with peers — whether it be a bashful look, an unobtrusive token of consideration or prohibition, or the elements of gathering play — offer important experiences into their social turn of events. Understanding these signs can help grown-ups in establishing strong conditions that cultivate positive social communications and profound development.

The meaning of ignored prompts in kids' way of behaving turns out to be considerably more articulated with regards to youth training and formative brain research. Teachers, furnished with a consciousness of the subtleties of life as a youngster conduct, assume an essential part in establishing conditions that sustain comprehensive turn of events. By being receptive to the ignored prompts in a study hall setting, teachers can tailor their ways to deal with oblige the special necessities of every youngster, cultivating a learning climate that is both comprehensive and receptive to individual contrasts.

In the domain of formative brain research, the idea of neglected signals lines up with the more extensive comprehension of youngsters as dynamic members in their own turn of events.

The persuasive hypotheses of analysts, for example, Vygotsky and Piaget highlight the significance of perceiving kids as specialists of their picking up, underscoring the job of social connections and play in mental and profound turn of events. By recognizing and deciphering the disregarded signs inside these unique circumstances, clinicians can add to a more far reaching comprehension of the unpredictable cycles that shape a kid's development.

The investigation of disregarded signals in kids' way of behaving is an excursion that requests an all encompassing comprehension of the horde impacts molding a kid's reality. Past the prompt associations inside the family or instructive settings, cultural and social variables add to the arrangement of these signs. The idea of neglected prompts coaxes us to dig into the more extensive material of a youngster's current circumstance, perceiving the complex idea of their encounters.

Culture assumes a significant part in molding the standards, values, and assumptions that encompass youngsters. Each culture has its novel approaches to communicating feelings, cultivating freedom, and exploring social connections. Disregarded signals in a multicultural setting might appear as varieties in correspondence styles, ways to deal with discipline, or the accentuation put on individual versus aggregate character. Understanding these social subtleties is fundamental for guardians and teachers, as it permits them to decipher the unpretentious signs in a way that lines up with the social setting, staying away from misinterpretations and encouraging a more comprehensive climate.

Besides, the idea of disregarded signals crosses with the developing consciousness of neurodiversity — an acknowledgment of the different manners by which people's minds capability. Neurodivergent kids, including conditions, for example, chemical imbalance range turmoil, ADHD, or tangible handling issues, may display remarkable signs that require a specific comprehension. Ignored prompts in neurodivergent kids could incorporate aversions to tactile upgrades, explicit correspondence inclinations, or unmistakable examples of commitment in play. By embracing neurodiversity and tuning into these nuanced signals, parental figures and teachers can offer custom fitted help that regards the independence of every youngster.

Innovation, in its ubiquity, likewise acquaints an original aspect with the idea of ignored signals. Kids, experiencing childhood in a computerized period, draw in with screens, gadgets, and virtual conditions since the beginning. Disregarded signs in this setting might appear as changes in screen time conduct, inclinations for specific computerized exercises, or the close to home effect of online communications. Understanding the ramifications of innovation on a kid's improvement is urgent for guardians and teachers, as it empowers them to explore the computerized scene in a manner that lines up with the youngster's prosperity and generally speaking development.

Moreover, the job of parental impact couldn't possibly be more significant in that frame of mind of disregarded prompts. Guardians, as essential parental figures, shape the early encounters and impression of kids. Ignored prompts inside the relational intricacy might include the implicit messages passed on through parental connections, the displaying of close to home guideline, or the effect of parental weight on a kid's prosperity. By inspecting these prompts, guardians can encourage a sustaining home climate that advances profound flexibility, sound connection, and open correspondence.

In the instructive circle, the idea of ignored signals is unpredictably connected to the advancing standards of educating and learning. Conventional instructive models frequently focus on scholarly accomplishments, some of the time disregarding the social and profound components of a kid's turn of events. Ignored signals in the homeroom might incorporate unobtrusive articulations of scholarly pressure, challenges in peer connections, or signs of neglected profound requirements. Instructive experts, by adjusting themselves to these signs, can carry out all encompassing methodologies that address the complex idea of a kid's development, encouraging a decent and steady learning climate.

The job of play, as a foundation of experience growing up, becomes the dominant focal point in the investigation of disregarded prompts. Play isn't just a mode for diversion yet a powerful field where kids arrange social jobs, express inventiveness, and trial with critical thinking. Neglected prompts inside the domain of play could include deviations from average play designs, the rise of innovative subjects reflecting unsaid wants, or the elements of helpful play. By unraveling these prompts, guardians and instructors can acquire significant experiences into the mental, close to home, and social elements of a kid's turn of events, making ready for deliberate and designated help.

In the more extensive setting of youngster backing, the idea of ignored signs pushes us to rethink cultural designs and approaches that influence kids. Issues like neediness, segregation, and deficient admittance to medical services can appear in the ignored signals of kids — whether it be formative postponements, conduct difficulties, or profound pain. Kid backers and policymakers, by recognizing and tending to these prompts, can pursue making fundamental changes that guarantee each youngster has the valuable chance to flourish in a strong and fair climate.

The multifacetedness of disregarded signals likewise embraces the gendered encounters of youngsters. Cultural assumptions and generalizations frequently impact how young men and young ladies put themselves out there, explore connections, and draw in with their environmental factors. Neglected signs in gendered settings might include the unpretentious support of orientation standards in play, the effect of media depictions on self-discernment, or the nuanced manners by which kids explore peer communications. By perceiving and testing these gendered signals, guardians and teachers add to establishing conditions that enable kids to communicate their uniqueness past prohibitive generalizations.

The idea of neglected signs in youngsters' conduct welcomes us to leave on an exhaustive investigation that reaches out past the prompt collaborations of family and schooling. It incorporates social, neurodiversity, mechanical, parental, instructive, and cultural aspects, recognizing the interconnected web that shapes a youngster's reality. By unraveling these prompts, we open a more profound comprehension of a youngster's necessities, feelings, and formative directions. The idea of disregarded signs fills in as a source of inspiration for parental figures, teachers, policymakers, and backers to team up in establishing conditions that commend the uniqueness of every kid and offer the essential help for their all encompassing development and prospering.

1.2 Exploring the subtle signals children emit that often go unnoticed.

In the complex embroidery of experience growing up, where guiltlessness and interest dance connected at the hip, there exists a domain of unobtrusive signs radiated by kids — signals that frequently slip by everyone's notice in the midst of the extravagance of their play and the motion of day to day existence. This investigation looks to disentangle the puzzle of these ignored prompts, diving into the profundities of kids' ways of behaving to divulge the quiet language they utilize to communicate wants, fears, and neglected needs.

One of the central areas where these unobtrusive signs manifest is in the subtleties of nonverbal correspondence. Kids, particularly in their early stages, may not have the created jargon to exhaustively express their contemplations and feelings. Hence, their interior universes track down demeanor through nonverbal means, like looks, non-verbal communication, and motions. The wrinkled forehead, the downturned look, or the squirming fingers — all are components of a quiet story that, when interpreted, gives a window into the youngster's close to home scene.

These nonverbal prompts frequently act as a demonstration of the kid's personal prosperity. For example, an unexpected change in nonverbal communication from open and loose to shut and tense might show distress, uneasiness, or a sensation of weakness. On the other hand, the unobtrusive shimmer in a kid's eye, the skip in their step, or the unguarded chuckling might mean happiness, satisfaction, and a feeling that everything is good. Perceiving and deciphering these nonverbal signs permits guardians, guardians, and instructors to answer sympathetically to a youngster's feelings, establishing a steady climate that cultivates the capacity to understand individuals on a deeper level.

The elements of play, a basic piece of experience growing up, likewise structure a material on which these disregarded signs are painted. Play isn't simply a paltry side interest; it is a medium through which youngsters figure out the world, try different things with jobs, and cycle their feelings.

In the kaleidoscope of play, unobtrusive signs might arise as deviations from regular play designs, inclinations for explicit toys or exercises, or the consolidation of topics that reflect basic cravings or fears. By submerging themselves in the realm of an easy breezy, grown-ups can acquire significant bits of knowledge into the kid's creative mind and profound scene.

Consider a kid immersed in lone play, orchestrating toys fastidiously or participating in dull activities. These apparently dull ways of behaving can be ignored signals characteristic of the youngster's requirement for schedule, consistency, or a type of self-calming. On the other hand, a kid who reliably presents subjects of salvage or security in their play might be unobtrusively flagging a craving for consolation and security. By understanding the language of play, parental figures and teachers can reveal these signals and designer their help to address the remarkable requirements rising up out of the youngster's innovative world.

Changes in conduct, both unpretentious and articulated, likewise act as signs on the excursion of experience growing up advancement. As kids explore the perplexing landscape of feelings, connections, and self-disclosure, their way of behaving turns into an impression of their inward states. The ignored signals in social movements could appear as withdrawal, animosity, tenacity, or changes in rest designs. For example, a formerly cordial kid who becomes held or a normally quiet kid displaying eruptions of disappointment might be flagging a close to home battle or a requirement for extra help.

Investigating these conduct signs requires a nuanced comprehension of the singular kid. Factors like personality, formative stage, and outer stressors all assume a part in shaping a youngster's way of behaving. By moving toward social changes with interest and sympathy, guardians can uncover the tales behind the signals, giving the vital framework to a kid to successfully explore difficulties and articulate their thoughts.

The social elements of experience growing up, including collaborations with peers and the more extensive local area, offer one more aspect to the investigation of disregarded signals. Kids are not separated substances but rather dynamic members in a social biological system where they find out about cooperation, compassion, and the complexities of connections. Unobtrusive signs in friendly communications might incorporate a bashful look, a reluctant move toward consideration, or the unpretentious subtleties of overall vibes during play.

Understanding the expressive gestures in youngsters' way of behaving requires a sharp consciousness of the frequently implicit principles of commitment. A youngster who reliably positions themselves on the outskirts of gathering play might be flagging sensations of rejection or vulnerability about friendly elements. Then again, a youngster who effectively looks for open doors for joint effort and exhibits compassion towards companions might be communicating a craving for association and positive social commitment. By interpreting these neglected signs, guardians and instructors can work with a comprehensive climate that supports solid social turn of events.

The coming of innovation, with its unavoidable presence in contemporary society, presents an original scene for investigating ignored prompts in kids' way of behaving. Kids, from an exceptionally youthful age, draw in with computerized gadgets, screens, and virtual conditions. Ignored signals in the advanced domain might appear as changes in screen time conduct, inclinations for explicit computerized exercises, or close to home reactions to online collaborations. For instance, an unexpected hesitance to participate in disconnected exercises, over the top connection to computerized gadgets, or indications of trouble during or after web-based cooperations can be unpretentious signs that warrant consideration.

The advanced scene presents the two potential open doors and difficulties for grasping kids' ways of behaving. On one hand, innovation gives new roads to learning, inventiveness, and social association. Then again, it presents expected dangers and effects on prosperity. By exploring the computerized domain with mindfulness and open correspondence, parental figures can decipher these ignored prompts, guaranteeing a decent and solid connection among kids and innovation.

Parental impact, as an unavoidable power in a kid's life, shapes the underpinning of many ignored prompts. The nuclear family fills in as the essential setting where kids initially find out about connections, correspondence, and profound articulation. The disregarded prompts inside the relational peculiarity might include the implicit messages passed on through parental collaborations, the displaying of close to home guideline, and the effect of familial weight on a youngster's prosperity.

Consider a situation where guardians, overpowered by outside pressures, unintentionally pass pressure or nervousness on through their activities and articulations. The youngster, receptive to these neglected signals, may retain the close to home strain without the capacity to expressly verbalize their sentiments. This assimilation of parental pressure can appear in different ways, like changes in conduct, rest aggravations, or a general feeling of disquiet. Perceiving these disregarded signs inside the nuclear family prompts guardians and guardians to participate in open correspondence, cultivating a sincerely strong climate for the youngster.

In the instructive circle, the idea of ignored signs stretches out to the elements of the study hall and the advancing standards of educating and learning. Conventional instructive models frequently focus on scholarly accomplishments, possibly sidelining the social and close to home components of a kid's turn of events. Disregarded signs in the homeroom might incorporate unobtrusive articulations of scholastic pressure, challenges in peer communications, or signs of neglected profound necessities.

Instructive experts, by adjusting themselves to these signs, can carry out comprehensive methodologies that address the multi-layered nature of a youngster's development. For example, a youngster who reliably exhibits indications of scholastic pressure might profit from extra help or elective learning systems.

Besides, ignored signals might direct teachers in perceiving the novel qualities and interests of every youngster, considering separated guidance that praises individual learning styles.

The investigation of disregarded signals in youngsters' way of behaving converges with the developing consciousness of neurodiversity — an acknowledgment of the different manners by which people's cerebrums capability. Neurodivergent youngsters, including conditions, for example, chemical imbalance range turmoil, ADHD, or tangible handling issues, may show one of a kind signs that require a particular comprehension. Ignored signals in neurodivergent youngsters could incorporate aversions to tactile upgrades, explicit correspondence inclinations, or unmistakable examples of commitment in play.

Embracing neurodiversity and tuning into these nuanced signs permits parental figures and instructors to offer custom fitted help that regards the uniqueness of every kid. For instance, a kid with tactile responsive qualities might show prompts like repugnances for specific surfaces, evasion of uproarious conditions, or looking for explicit tangible info. Perceiving and answering these prompts empowers the production of conditions that oblige neurodivergent needs, encouraging a feeling of inclusivity and understanding.

The all-encompassing investigation of neglected prompts in kids' way of behaving is indivisible from the more extensive sociocultural setting that shapes the accounts of life as a youngster. Culture, with its complex embroidered artwork of standards, values, and assumptions, impacts how youngsters articulate their thoughts, explore connections, and see the world. Ignored signs inside social settings might appear as varieties in correspondence styles, ways to deal with discipline, or the accentuation put on individual versus aggregate character.

Perceiving these social subtleties is fundamental for parental figures and teachers, as it permits them to decipher the unpretentious signs in a way that lines up with the social setting, keeping away from misinterpretations and cultivating a more comprehensive climate. For example, a youngster from a culture that values cooperation might show signs like areas of strength for a for bunch exercises or elevated aversion to social elements. Understanding these social signs permits grown-ups to offer help that regards and praises assorted social foundations.

In the investigation of disregarded signals, the gendered encounters of kids arise as another basic feature. Cultural assumptions and generalizations frequently impact how young men and young ladies put themselves out there, explore connections, and draw in with their environmental factors. Ignored prompts in gendered settings might include the unpretentious support of orientation standards in play, the effect of media depictions on self-discernment, or the nuanced manners by which kids explore peer communications.

Consider a situation where a little fellow, impacted by cultural assumptions, stifles his feelings to adjust to customary manly standards.

The neglected signs in this present circumstance might incorporate unobtrusive articulations of profound limitation, hesitance to take part in sustaining play, or the concealing of weakness. Perceiving and testing these gendered signals permits parental figures and teachers to establish conditions that enable kids to communicate their uniqueness past prohibitive generalizations.

The diversity of disregarded signs likewise recognizes the job of foundational factors in molding youngsters' encounters. Issues like destitution, segregation, and lacking admittance to medical care can appear in the neglected signals of kids — whether it be formative deferrals, conduct difficulties, or close to home pain. Youngster backers and policymakers, by recognizing and tending to these signs, can pursue making fundamental changes that guarantee each kid has the potential chance to flourish in a steady and evenhanded climate.

As we dive further into the investigation of neglected prompts in youngsters' way of behaving, it becomes obvious that the comprehension of these unobtrusive signs is entwined with the advancing scene of formative brain research. The hypotheses and points of view inside this field give a system to deciphering the nuanced prompts youngsters transmit, offering experiences into the intricacies of their mental, close to home, and social turn of events.

Jean Piaget, a trailblazer in the field of formative brain research, proposed a hypothesis of mental improvement that underlines the significance of the kid's dynamic commitment with their current circumstance. Piaget's phases of mental turn of events — sensorimotor, preoperational, concrete functional, and formal functional — offer a focal point through which to look at the disregarded signals in kids' way of behaving. For instance, a youngster in the sensorimotor stage might show prompts through exploratory ways of behaving, while a kid in the preoperational stage might display emblematic play for of offering inside viewpoints and feelings.

Lev Vygotsky, one more powerful figure in formative brain science, presented the sociocultural hypothesis that features the job of social connections and social impacts in mental turn of events. Vygotsky's idea of the zone of proximal turn of events (ZPD) recommends that learning happens inside the scope of what a kid can do freely and what they can accomplish with the help of a more educated person. Ignored prompts in friendly cooperations, peer connections, and social settings can be grasped from the perspective of Vygotsky's hypothesis, underlining the significance of these outer impacts on a youngster's turn of events.

Connection hypothesis, spearheaded by John Bowlby, offers one more layer to our investigation of disregarded prompts. Bowlby's hypothesis highlights the meaning of early parental figure kid connections in molding profound and social turn of events.

Ignored signs inside connection elements might include the unpretentious articulations of a protected connection, for example, a kid certainly investigating their current circumstance and looking for vicinity to a guardian when required. Conversely, signs demonstrative of an unreliable connection could appear as tenacity, evasion, or trouble framing associations with others.

Erik Erikson's psychosocial hypothesis presents the idea of phases of psychosocial improvement, each related with a particular formative test. Neglected signs in kids' way of behaving may line up with the difficulties of Erikson's stages, for example, the independence versus disgrace and uncertainty stage during toddlerhood, where signals could be communicated through a youngster's blossoming feeling of freedom or reluctance in championing themselves.

As we investigate the multifacetedness of ignored prompts and neurodiversity, it is fundamental to consider contemporary points of view on conditions, for example, chemical imbalance range jumble (ASD). The social model of handicap stresses the job of cultural boundaries in making handicap as opposed to crediting it exclusively to a singular's hindrances. With regards to disregarded signs in neurodivergent kids, understanding and obliging neurodiversity line up with the standards of inclusivity and the acknowledgment of different approaches to encountering and communicating oneself.

Inside the setting of innovation, Jean Twenge's work on the effect of computerized media on kids' way of behaving gives important experiences. The iGen age, brought into the world during the 1990s and later, has grown up drenched in cell phones and online entertainment. Neglected signs in this mechanical scene might include shifts in correspondence designs, the impact of virtual entertainment on self-discernment, or the possible effect of screen time on psychological well-being. Twenge's examination urges grown-ups to be sensitive to these disregarded signals, adjusting nurturing and instructive ways to deal with the special difficulties introduced by the computerized age.

The investigation of ignored signs converges with the expanding field of positive brain research, which looks to comprehend and elevate factors that add to a satisfying life. Positive brain science reveals insight into neglected prompts connected with prosperity, satisfaction, and flexibility in kids. For example, signs characteristic of positive mental improvement might incorporate articulations of appreciation, the limit with regards to compassion, and the capacity to explore difficulties with a development outlook. By perceiving and supporting these neglected signals, guardians and teachers add to the all encompassing improvement of youngsters past the customary spotlight on deficiencies or difficulties.

As we explore the intricacies of ignored signals in youngsters' way of behaving, the standards of injury informed care become progressively significant.

Injury informed care recognizes the commonness of unfavorable youth encounters and the possible effect of injury on a youngster's turn of events. Ignored signs connected with injury might incorporate hypervigilance, aversion of specific boosts, or difficulties in framing confiding in connections. An injury informed approach prompts grown-ups to move toward kids with responsiveness, perceiving and answering these signals in a way that advances security, trust, and recuperating.

With regards to instructive brain science, the idea of disregarded signs lines up with the standards of understudy focused learning and separated guidance. Understudy focused learning underscores fitting instructive encounters to meet the special necessities and interests of every understudy. Neglected signals in the study hall, whether connected with learning styles, inspiration, or close to home prosperity, brief teachers to move past normalized approaches and embrace a more customized and responsive instructional method.

Moreover, the investigation of ignored signals in kids' conduct requires a reconsideration of appraisal and assessment rehearses inside instructive settings. The accentuation on state sanctioned testing and grades might eclipse the abundance of data implanted in the unpretentious signs kids transmit. Elective types of appraisal, for example, project-based evaluations, portfolios, and story assessments, give a more far reaching perspective on a kid's assets, difficulties, and exceptional characteristics, lining up with the standards of perceiving and esteeming disregarded signs.

In the more extensive domain of emotional well-being, the convergence of neglected signals and versatility features the significance of encouraging versatile survival techniques in kids. Versatility, the capacity to quickly return from misfortune, is a significant figure kids' prosperity. Neglected prompts connected with strength might include a youngster's ability for critical thinking, looking for social help, or using positive survival techniques. Perceiving and supporting these disregarded signs adds to the development of close to home flexibility, furnishing youngsters with the apparatuses to explore life's difficulties.

The investigation of disregarded signs likewise crosses with the field of social brain science, underscoring the significance of figuring out conduct inside social settings. Social therapists perceive that standards, values, and assumptions fluctuate across societies, affecting how people articulate their thoughts and explore social collaborations. Disregarded signals inside social settings might include varieties in correspondence styles, articulations of cooperation or independence, and the effect of social stories on a youngster's feeling of personality. By embracing social variety and social capability, guardians and teachers can decipher and answer these signs in a way that regards and praises different social foundations.

The excursion into the universe of ignored signs in kids' way of behaving is enhanced by drawing upon assorted points of view inside the domain of brain science. From essential hypotheses of mental and psychosocial improvement to contemporary structures, for example, positive brain science, injury informed care, and understudy focused learning, every point of view adds to an exhaustive comprehension of the multi-layered nature of experience growing up.

Besides, the acknowledgment of disregarded signals inside the interconnection of neurodiversity, innovation, versatility, and social variety highlights the significance of moving toward kids with a receptive outlook and a promise to inclusivity. By embracing these different points of view, parental figures, teachers, policymakers, and supporters can explore the intricacies of experience growing up with a nuanced comprehension of the quiet language kids use to convey their cravings, fears, and neglected needs. The incorporation of these mental viewpoints gives a comprehensive system to establishing conditions that honor the extravagance of life as a youngster and advance the prosperity and thriving of each and every kid.

1.3 Anecdotes and real-life examples illustrating the significance of these cues.

Tales and genuine models strikingly represent the significant meaning of ignored prompts in youngsters' way of behaving, rejuvenating the unpretentious signs that frequently slip through the cracks. These accounts embody the extravagance of the quiet language kids use to convey their longings, fears, and neglected needs, underlining the significance of attunement and responsiveness from parental figures, instructors, and the more extensive local area.

Think about the narrative of Emily, a six-year-old entering her most memorable year of formal training. By all accounts, she had all the earmarks of being a lively and friendly youngster, drawing in with her companions during recess and partaking in study hall exercises. Nonetheless, her educator, Mrs. Johnson, saw unpretentious signs in Emily's way of behaving that alluded to hidden difficulties. During bunch exercises, Emily frequently wondered whether or not to make some noise or express her thoughts, liking to mix away from plain sight. Interestingly, her drawings and fine art uncovered a rich internal world, loaded up with perplexing subtleties and dynamic tones.

Perceiving these ignored prompts, Mrs. Johnson started a discussion with Emily, making a place of refuge for her to share her considerations and sentiments. Through this exchange, Emily uncovered her vulnerability about talking before the class, dreading judgment and dismissal from her companions.

Mrs. Johnson's mindfulness of the unobtrusive prompts in Emily's conduct empowered her to offer designated help, empowering Emily to articulate her thoughts through elective means, like sharing her thoughts in little gatherings or utilizing composed correspondence. After some time, Emily's certainty bloomed, and the ignored signals turned into a pathway for her to explore the social intricacies of the study hall.

The tale of Jake, a ten-year-old enthusiastically for narrating, further shows the meaning of ignored prompts inside the setting of play. Jake, notwithstanding his extravagance during inventive play meetings, reliably integrated subjects of flexibility, defeating difficulties, and valor into his accounts. His instructor, Mrs. Rodriguez, perceived these unpretentious signs as marks of a more profound close to home scene. Upon additional investigation, it became apparent that Jake was wrestling with sensations of weakness connected with changes in his relational peculiarities.

Mrs. Rodriguez utilized the force of narrating to make a restorative space for Jake, permitting him to externalize his feelings and investigate valuable stories. By recognizing and answering the neglected prompts implanted in Jake's creative play, Mrs. Rodriguez gave a steady outlet to him to handle his feelings and foster survival strategies. The disregarded signals, communicated with the help of play, turned into an impetus for Jake's personal versatility and prosperity.

In the domain of innovation, the narrative of Lily, a thirteen-year-old exploring the intricacies of web-based entertainment, reveals insight into the ignored signs connected with computerized cooperations. Lily, an eager client of different social stages, showed a huge change in her web-based conduct, set apart by expanded withdrawal and a hesitance to share individual encounters. Her folks, receptive to these ignored signals, started a discussion with Lily to figure out the fundamental elements.

As Lily drilled down into her encounters, it became clear that she was wrestling with cyberbullying and online antagonism. The neglected prompts in her computerized conduct filled in as marks of close to home misery and the requirement for help. Lily's folks, furnished with a comprehension of the meaning of these signs, teamed up with her to explore the difficulties of the advanced scene. They carried out systems to upgrade Lily's web-based prosperity, encouraging open correspondence and versatility even with online misfortune.

The story of Alex, a neurodivergent youngster determined to have chemical imbalance range jumble (ASD), gives a piercing illustration of the diversity between neglected signals and neurodiversity. Alex, at seven years old, battled with advances and changes in daily schedule, frequently prompting total implosions and elevated nervousness. His educator, Mr. Thompson, perceived these neglected prompts as indications of tactile responsive qualities and the requirement for an organized climate.

Accordingly, Mr. Thompson teamed up with Alex's folks to make a custom-made learning plan that obliged his remarkable necessities. By integrating tactile breaks, visual timetables, and clear correspondence techniques, Mr. Thompson changed ignored prompts into open doors for development and learning. Alex's excursion inside the instructive setting turned into a demonstration of the extraordinary force of perceiving and answering the neglected signs related with neurodiversity.

The tale of Mia, a twelve-year-old exploring the intricacies of social personality, embodies what ignored signals inside social settings mean for a youngster's identity. Mia, brought into the world to outsider guardians, wrestled with a feeling of uprooting and attempted to accommodate the assumptions for her social legacy with the more extensive cultural standards. Through unpretentious signals in her specialty, composing, and articulations of personality, Mia conveyed her unseen struggles to her educator, Ms. Patel.

Ms. Patel, receptive to these disregarded signals, started discussions that permitted Mia to investigate her social character in a steady climate. By encouraging a comprehensive homeroom that commended variety, Ms. Patel changed the ignored signals connected with Mia's social encounters into potential open doors for multifaceted comprehension and self-acknowledgment. Mia's process turned into a demonstration of the significant effect of perceiving and embracing neglected prompts inside the mind boggling embroidery of social impacts.

The story of Ethan, a nine-year-old exploring the difficulties of parental separation, reveals insight into the neglected signals inserted inside relational intricacies. Ethan, at first a fiery and scholastically connected with kid, started showing signals, for example, changes in rest designs, a decrease in scholarly execution, and expanded profound responsiveness. His instructor, Mrs. Turner, perceived these ignored prompts as expected signs of close to home misery connected with his family circumstance.

Mrs. Turner teamed up with the school guide to establish a steady climate for Ethan. By giving open doors to articulation through craftsmanship treatment and encouraging open correspondence channels, they recognized and answered the ignored prompts exuding from Ethan's encounters. This approach worked with his close to home handling and flexibility, showing the groundbreaking effect of perceiving and tending to disregarded signals inside the setting of family challenges.

The story of Aiden, a fifteen-year-old exploring the gendered assumptions for immaturity, features the neglected signals connected with orientation personality. Aiden, doled out female upon entering the world, unpretentiously communicated signs connected with uneasiness with relegated orientation jobs and a craving for self-articulation that lined up with a male orientation character. Perceiving these disregarded prompts, Aiden's school advisor, Ms. Taylor, made a safe and insisting space for open discussions about orientation personality and articulation.

Through continuous help and promotion, Ms. Taylor engaged Aiden to explore the intricacies of orientation character inside the instructive setting. The disregarded signals connected with Aiden's orientation process turned into an impetus for encouraging inclusivity and figuring out inside the school local area. Aiden's story highlights the extraordinary force of perceiving and regarding neglected signals with regards to orientation variety.

The tale of Noah, a six-year-old exploring the repercussions of a horrible mishap, embodies the interconnection of ignored signals and injury informed care. Noah, having seen a horrible episode in his area, showed prompts like uplifted tension, withdrawal, and relapse in formative achievements. His kindergarten instructor, Ms. Lewis, perceived these disregarded signals as marks of injury and started an injury informed way to deal with help Noah.

Ms. Lewis teamed up with the school guide and Noah's folks to establish a protected and unsurprising climate for him. By consolidating injury informed procedures, like tactile backings, profound guideline methods, and a supporting daily practice, they changed ignored signs connected with injury into valuable open doors for mending and versatility. Noah's process turned into a demonstration of the groundbreaking effect of injury educated care and the acknowledgment regarding neglected signals with regards to misfortune.

These genuine models highlight the urgent job of guardians, teachers, and the more extensive local area in perceiving and answering the ignored signals implanted in kids' way of behaving. Every account features the extraordinary force of attunement, compassion, and deliberate help in opening the possible inside disregarded signals. Whether inside the domains of play, innovation, neurodiversity, social variety, relational intricacies, orientation personality, or injury, the accounts of these youngsters enlighten the multifaceted embroidered artwork of experience growing up and the significant effect of understanding and esteeming the quiet language they use to impart their inward universes.

The investigation of ignored signals in youngsters' way of behaving reaches out past individual tales to envelop more extensive cultural accounts that shape the encounters of kids. These stories enlighten the interconnected trap of impacts, difficulties, and open doors that add to the quiet language kids use to convey their cravings, fears, and neglected needs.

Think about the story of Sophie, a ten-year-old exploring the intricacies of neediness inside the setting of disregarded signals. Sophie's family confronted monetary difficulties that appeared in neglected signs like changes in her school participation, a decrease in scholarly execution, and articulations of craving. The prompts connected with neediness, frequently undetectable to those uninformed about the more extensive setting, flagged difficulties in addressing essential necessities and getting to instructive assets.

Sophie's story highlights the meaning of perceiving and addressing the cultural variables that add to ignored signals in youngsters' way of behaving. Destitution, with its extensive ramifications, can influence a kid's prosperity, instructive open doors, and close to home strength. By recognizing the neglected signs related with financial difficulties, policymakers and promoters can pursue making foundational changes that address the main drivers of neediness and guarantee evenhanded admittance to assets for each youngster.

The story of Javier, a twelve-year-old exploring the difficulties of segregation and social personality, reveals insight into the ignored prompts inside the interconnection of social variety and cultural assumptions. Javier, an offspring of foreigner guardians, confronted separation in view of his social foundation, prompting signals, for example, a hesitance to take part in school exercises and a reduced identity worth. These neglected prompts reflected the more extensive cultural stories that propagated generalizations and predispositions.

Perceiving and testing the cultural elements adding to ignored signals connected with segregation turns into a critical part of establishing comprehensive conditions for youngsters. By cultivating social ability, advancing variety schooling, and destroying oppressive designs, society can add to a climate where each kid feels esteemed, seen, and allowed to communicate their novel character unafraid of judgment or predisposition.

The story of Maya, a fourteen-year-old exploring the effect of media depictions on self-perception, features the ignored signs installed inside cultural assumptions around excellence norms. Maya, besieged by romanticized pictures in media, showed prompts, for example, negative self-perception, low confidence, and commitment to undesirable slimming down ways of behaving. These neglected signals mirrored the unavoidable impact of media stories on a kid's impression of self-esteem and excellence.

The cultural account encompassing self-perception and magnificence principles highlights the requirement for media education and the advancement of positive portrayals. By testing unreasonable depictions in media, advancing different self-perceptions, and encouraging discussions around confidence, society can add to a more strong climate where kids are enabled to embrace their one of a kind bodies and characters without surrendering to unsafe cultural tensions.

The story of Caleb, a sixteen-year-old exploring the intricacies of emotional well-being inside the schooling system, points out the ignored prompts connected with scholarly pressure and the shame encompassing psychological wellness. Caleb, showing signals, for example, withdrawal, changes in rest examples, and scholastic burnout, mirrored the more extensive cultural story that frequently focuses on scholarly accomplishments over mental prosperity.

The cultural assumption for scholarly achievement can add to ignored signals in youngsters' way of behaving, demonstrating basic stressors that might slip through the cracks. By encouraging a culture of prosperity inside instructive foundations, focusing on psychological well-being schooling, and destigmatizing looking for help, society can add to a climate where kids feel upheld in exploring the tensions related with scholarly execution.

The story of Olivia, a seventeen-year-old exploring the intricacies of companion connections and web-based entertainment, highlights the disregarded signs connected with the effect of cyberbullying and online tensions. Olivia, showing signals like expanded social withdrawal, profound misery, and hesitance to participate in web-based stages, reflected the more extensive cultural account encompassing the difficulties of exploring social collaborations in the advanced age.

Society assumes an essential part in tending to the disregarded signals related with the computerized scene. By advancing computerized citizenship, cultivating compassion in web-based collaborations, and executing viable enemy of cyberbullying measures, society can establish a climate where kids can explore the advanced world with flexibility, positive social associations, and a feeling of safety.

The story of Elijah, an eighteen-year-old exploring the difficulties of progressing into adulthood inside the child care framework, features the ignored signals related with fundamental issues in kid government assistance. Elijah, showing signs, for example, hardships in shaping stable connections, an apprehension about maturing out of the framework, and an absence of groundwork for free living, mirrored the more extensive cultural story that frequently neglects to offer sufficient help for youngsters changing out of child care.

Perceiving and addressing the foundational factors adding to ignored signals in the child care framework turns into a cultural objective. By upholding for extensive emotionally supportive networks, mentorship programs, and instructive assets for youth in child care, society can add to a more impartial and strong climate for youngsters changing into adulthood.

The story of Isabella, a nineteen-year-old exploring the difficulties of LGBTQ+ personality inside familial and cultural settings, features the neglected signals connected with the requirement for acknowledgment and confirmation. Isabella, showing signals, for example, a hesitance to reveal her character, profound misery, and stressed family connections, mirrored the more extensive cultural story encompassing the LGBTQ+ people group, where acknowledgment and understanding are in many cases thwarted by social and cultural predispositions.

Tending to the ignored prompts related with LGBTQ+ character requires cultural movements towards inclusivity, acknowledgment, and instruction. By cultivating conditions that embrace variety, testing unfair practices, and advancing LGBTQ+ perceivability, society can add to a really certifying and strong space for youngsters exploring their personalities.

These accounts highlight the interconnectedness of neglected signs in youngsters' way of behaving with more extensive cultural stories. The narratives of Sophie, Javier, Maya, Caleb, Olivia, Elijah, and Isabella enlighten the significant effect of cultural assumptions, segregation, media impacts, emotional well-being shame, the advanced scene, child care framework challenges, and LGBTQ+ acknowledgment on the encounters of youngsters.

Perceiving and tending to these cultural variables is fundamental for establishing conditions that sustain the prosperity, flexibility, and novel characters of each and every kid. The source of inspiration stretches out to policymakers, instructors, guardians, and networks to effectively add to cultural movements that encourage inclusivity, value, and understanding. By recognizing and answering the disregarded signals inside the bigger cultural setting, we prepare for a more empathetic and steady existence where each kid can prosper and flourish.

Chapter 2

The Language They Speak

The language verbally expressed by kids, frequently quiet and nuanced, rises above the bounds of words. It is an embroidery woven with inconspicuous prompts, signals, and ways of behaving that comprise a rich and complex story. This quiet language, extraordinary to every kid, fills in as a window into their inward world, communicating wants, fears, and neglected needs. Understanding the language they talk requires a profound jump into the unpredictable elements of young life, enveloping the domains of feelings, play, social collaborations, and the impact of outer variables.

In the area of feelings, the language kids talk is overwhelmingly nonverbal. From the earliest phases of outset, before the securing of language, infants convey through cries, looks, and body developments. The mindful parental figure becomes capable at unraveling these prompts, recognizing an eager cry and a drained one, or perceiving the unpretentious articulations of satisfaction or distress. As kids develop, their close to home jargon grows, however the nonverbal prompts stay a critical part of their correspondence.

Looks act as an essential channel for the statement of feelings. The wrinkled temple of a kid wrestling with disarray, the brilliant grin reflecting satisfaction, or the downturned look showing bitterness — these are components of the quiet language youngsters use to convey their close to home states. Besides, the eyes, frequently alluded to as the windows to the spirit, offer a brief look into the profundity of a kid's sentiments. A sparkle of energy, a look deflected in timidity, or a watchful eye communicating assurance — all add to the rich embroidery of profound articulation.

Non-verbal communication, one more indispensable part of the quiet language, conveys volumes about a youngster's close to home prosperity. The drooped shoulders of a blue youngster, the enlivened tokens of an energized narrator, or the unobtrusive squirming reflecting anxiety — all convey feelings that might go implicit. Noticing these nonverbal prompts permits guardians, guardians, and teachers to adjust themselves to the feelings of the youngster, encouraging a steady climate that supports the capacity to understand people on a profound level.

The language kids talk through play is a dynamic and multi-layered articulation of their internal universes. Play, a long way from being a silly interest, fills in as a medium through which youngsters figure out their encounters, investigate jobs, and cycle feelings. The quiet language inside the domain of play is rich with signs that might slip through the cracks without cautious perception.

Consider a gathering of youngsters took part in inventive play, making situations and stories that mirror how they might interpret the world. The elements of force, participation, and struggle inside these play situations offer experiences into the social and profound elements at play. A kid who reliably assumes the job of a guardian or defender might be communicating a requirement for consolation and security. Then again, a youngster who investigates subjects of salvage or conquering difficulties might be handling their own encounters of versatility and adapting.

The language expressed through play is additionally clear in the inclinations and decisions youngsters make. The particular toys they float towards, the subjects they integrate into their play, or the characters they relate to — all add to the quiet account of their inward world. A disregarded prompt in a youngster's inclination for single play, for example, may mean a requirement for thoughtfulness or a snapshot of calm reflection in the midst of the lively social cooperations of experience growing up.

Changes in play examples can likewise be demonstrative of basic feelings or encounters. A kid who regularly participates in helpful play however out of nowhere pulls out into single exercises might be flagging a requirement for individual space or handling feelings freely. Perceiving these unobtrusive changes in play conduct permits parental figures and teachers to offer custom fitted help, establishing a climate that praises the kid's advancing necessities.

The social collaborations of young life structure one more element of the quiet language kids talk. From early connections with guardians to the complicated elements of companion connections, kids explore a social scene that shapes how they might interpret having a place, compassion, and correspondence. The quiet prompts inside these connections frequently manifest as varieties in correspondence styles, articulations of compassion, or marks of social solace or uneasiness.

Consider a youngster's dithering to join bunch exercises or draw in with peers. This neglected prompt might flag sensations of timidity, social tension, or vulnerability about the guidelines of commitment. Then again, a kid who effectively looks for potential open doors for coordinated effort, shows sympathy towards friends, or takes on positions of authority inside a gathering might be communicating a craving for association and positive social commitment.

The language verbally expressed through friendly cooperations is additionally apparent in the unobtrusive subtleties of correspondence. A youngster's manner of speaking, the utilization of motions, and the capacity to explore turn-taking in discussions all add to the quiet language that mirrors their social turn of events. A neglected prompt in a youngster's hesitance to visually engage or the reluctance in their discourse might give experiences into their solace level in group environments.

Understanding the quiet language of social collaborations requires a nuanced approach that thinks about the singularity of every kid. Factors like personality, social foundation, and past friendly encounters all assume a part in forming a youngster's correspondence style. By cultivating a climate that values different social articulations and empowering open correspondence, guardians and teachers can uphold kids in exploring the complexities of social collaborations.

The impact of outer elements on the quiet language youngsters talk couldn't possibly be more significant. The coming of innovation, with its unavoidable presence in contemporary society, presents an original scene for investigating disregarded signs in youngsters' way of behaving. Kids, from an exceptionally youthful age, draw in with computerized gadgets, screens, and virtual conditions, molding their encounters and articulations in special ways.

Ignored prompts in the advanced domain might appear as changes in screen time conduct, inclinations for explicit computerized exercises, or close to home reactions to online connections. A youngster who displays indications of pain during or after web-based connections, for instance, might be flagging the requirement for help in exploring the computerized scene. Then again, a youngster who reliably shows energy for inventive computerized exercises might be communicating a special type of articulation and investigation.

Exploring the computerized scene with mindfulness and open correspondence permits parental figures and instructors to actually decipher these ignored signals. It includes defining sound limits for screen time as well as participating in discussions that assist youngsters with articulating their encounters, inclinations, and worries in the advanced domain. Perceiving the quiet language of innovation enables grown-ups to direct youngsters in developing capable and positive advanced citizenship.

Parental impact, another outside factor forming the quiet language of youngsters, assumes a crucial part in their turn of events. The family climate, portrayed via providing care styles, correspondence designs, and the nature of connections, significantly impacts the quiet signals communicated by youngsters. Disregarded prompts inside the relational peculiarities might flag the effect of parental pressure, changes in family structure, or the requirement for extra help.

Consider the instance of a the youngster, amidst parental struggle, displays signals like withdrawal, changes in conduct, or articulations of nervousness. These ignored signs might mirror the profound effect of the family climate on the youngster's prosperity. Perceiving these signs prompts parental figures to address the main drivers of familial pressure, encouraging a steady climate that focuses on the feelings of the kid.

Parental association and correspondence styles additionally add to the quiet language spoken by youngsters. An ignored sign in a kid's hesitance to share encounters or examine feelings might demonstrate a requirement for a more open and strong correspondence channel inside the family. Setting out open doors for significant discussions, undivided attention, and common comprehension empowers guardians to unravel the quiet language of their kids and answer in a way that supports profound prosperity.

Instructive settings, incorporating the school climate and the elements of learning, are extra fields where the quiet language of kids unfurls. Disregarded signs inside instructive settings might appear as changes in scholarly execution, commitment levels, or articulations of dissatisfaction or weariness. Understanding these signs requires an all encompassing methodology that considers the different learning styles, inclinations, and individual necessities of every youngster.

Think about a kid who, regardless of showing scholarly capacities, shows signs of withdrawal or social difficulties in the homeroom. These ignored prompts might flag a misalignment between the kid's learning style and the instructive methodology. Perceiving these signs prompts teachers to embrace systems that take care of different learning modalities, encouraging a comprehensive climate that esteems every youngster's remarkable assets.

The quiet language of kids inside instructive settings is additionally obvious in their reactions to appraisals and assessments.

Ignored signs connected with test nervousness, execution pressure, or the effect of government sanctioned testing might appear as changes in conduct, close to home trouble, or a decrease in scholastic inspiration. Perceiving these signs prompts instructors to investigate elective evaluation strategies, cultivating a climate that values comprehensive learning and recognizes the assorted qualities of every youngster.

Neurodiversity, a characteristic part of human variety in mental working, acquaints one more layer with the quiet language spoken by youngsters. Disregarded prompts inside the domain of neurodiversity might appear as varieties in tangible awarenesses, correspondence styles, or the statement of one of a kind qualities and difficulties. Understanding and embracing the quiet language of neurodivergent youngsters requires a promise to inclusivity, compassion, and perceiving the worth of different approaches to encountering and communicating oneself.

Consider a youngster determined to have chemical imbalance range jumble (ASD) who showcases signals like an inclination for schedule, aversion to tangible boosts, or special types of correspondence. These neglected prompts, frequently misconstrued inside conventional systems, address the quiet language of neurodiversity. Perceiving and obliging these prompts permits guardians and instructors to establish conditions that honor the singularity of neurodivergent kids, cultivating a feeling of consideration and understanding.

Social impacts, profoundly implanted in the quiet language of kids, add to varieties in correspondence styles, articulations of character, and the forming of perspectives. Disregarded signals inside social settings might appear as varieties in play inclinations, ways to deal with social cooperations, or articulations of personality that reflect social qualities. Understanding these prompts requires social capability, a receptiveness to different viewpoints, and a pledge to establishing conditions that regard and celebrate social variety.

Consider a youngster from a multicultural foundation who, inside the school setting, shows signs, for example, an inclination for specific social exercises, varieties in correspondence styles, or articulations of character that mirror their social legacy. These disregarded signals offer experiences into the youngster's requirement for acknowledgment and assertion of their social character. Perceiving and answering these signals inside a socially capable system permits teachers and parental figures to establish comprehensive conditions that hug and praise the variety of social impacts.

Orientation elements, profoundly imbued in cultural accounts, add to the quiet language spoken by youngsters as they explore the intricacies of orientation personality and articulation. Ignored signals inside gendered settings might appear as varieties in play inclinations, articulations of orientation jobs, or signs of uneasiness with cultural assumptions.

Understanding the quiet language of orientation requires a consciousness of the effect of cultural standards and generalizations, and a guarantee to establishing conditions that engage kids to communicate their uniqueness past prohibitive orientation standards.

Consider a youngster who, impacted by cultural assumptions, displays signs like adherence to conventional orientation jobs, articulations of orientation dysphoria, or uneasiness with certain gendered exercises. These neglected signals mirror the quiet language of orientation elements, provoking guardians and teachers to encourage conditions that challenge generalizations, embrace orientation variety, and attest every youngster's novel personality.

The interconnection of ignored signs incorporates the more extensive sociocultural setting that shapes the stories of young life. Culture, with its unpredictable woven artwork of standards, values, and assumptions, impacts how youngsters articulate their thoughts, explore connections, and see the world. Ignored signals inside social settings might appear as varieties in correspondence styles, ways to deal with discipline, or the accentuation put on individual versus aggregate character.

Perceiving these social subtleties is fundamental for parental figures and teachers, as it permits them to decipher the unpretentious signs in a way that lines up with the social setting, keeping away from misinterpretations and cultivating a more comprehensive climate. For example, a youngster from a culture that values community might display prompts like areas of strength for a for bunch exercises or elevated aversion to social elements. Understanding these social signals permits grown-ups to offer help that regards and praises assorted social foundations.

In the investigation of ignored signals, the gendered encounters of kids arise as another basic feature. Cultural assumptions and generalizations frequently impact how young men and young ladies put themselves out there, explore connections, and draw in with their environmental elements. Ignored signs in gendered settings might include the unpretentious support of orientation standards in play, the effect of media depictions on self-discernment, or the nuanced manners by which youngsters explore peer cooperations.

Consider a situation where a young man, impacted by cultural assumptions, stifles his feelings to adjust to customary manly standards. The ignored signals in this present circumstance might incorporate unpretentious articulations of close to home limitation, hesitance to participate in sustaining play, or the covering of weakness. Perceiving and testing these gendered signals permits parental figures and teachers to establish conditions that enable kids to communicate their singularity past prohibitive generalizations.

The diversity of disregarded prompts additionally recognizes the job of fundamental elements in forming youngsters' encounters. Issues like neediness, separation, and deficient admittance to medical care can appear in the neglected signs of kids — whether it be formative postponements, conduct difficulties, or profound pain. Kid promoters and policymakers, by recognizing and tending to these prompts, can pursue making fundamental changes that guarantee each kid has the chance to flourish in a strong and impartial climate.

2.1 Delving into the unique communication style of children.

Digging into the novel correspondence style of youngsters divulges a universe of rich and nuanced articulation, rising above the traditional limits of language. Youngsters, in their early stages, explore a range of correspondence modes that envelop verbal and nonverbal signs, play cooperations, profound articulations, and the impact of outer variables. Understanding and valuing this unmistakable language requires a complete investigation that dives into the perplexing elements of life as a youngster correspondence.

At the center of kids' correspondence lies the domain of verbal articulation, where words become vessels for considerations, sentiments, and wants. Notwithstanding, the beginning phases of verbal correspondence are in many cases set apart by a progressive procurement of language abilities. Newborn children, in their pre-phonetic stage, impart principally through cries, coos, and prattling. The mindful guardian becomes sensitive to these nonverbal signals, answering the unpretentious subtleties of a child's vocalizations to address their issues for solace, sustenance, or consideration.

As kids progress through language improvement achievements, their verbal correspondence develops to envelop a developing jargon, sentence structure, and expressive capacities. However, even inside the domain of communicated in language, there exist varieties in correspondence styles that mirror the extraordinary characters, dispositions, and social impacts of every kid.

Consider the correspondence style of a gregarious and outgoing youngster who easily takes part in energized discussions, communicates thoughts with energy, and promptly collaborates with peers. This youngster's correspondence style mirrors an active and friendly nature, portrayed by an inclination for verbal articulation for the purpose of association and commitment.

Interestingly, a more contemplative and saved youngster might display a correspondence style set apart by insightful stops, particular word decisions, and an inclination for singular exercises. This kid's verbal articulations might be portrayed by profundity and thoughtfulness, mirroring a nuanced way to deal with correspondence that values reflection and individual space.

Perceiving and embracing the variety in youngsters' verbal correspondence styles is fundamental for guardians, teachers, and friends. It includes establishing conditions that celebrate various methods of articulation, encouraging a feeling of inclusivity where every youngster feels esteemed and comprehended. By recognizing the interesting characteristics of verbal correspondence, grown-ups can lay out significant associations with youngsters, empowering them to genuinely articulate their thoughts.

Nonverbal correspondence frames a significant part of the quiet language spoken by youngsters, uncovering bits of knowledge into their feelings, social communications, and tangible encounters. Looks, non-verbal communication, motions, and eye to eye connection comprise the nonverbal signals through which youngsters pass on a bunch of messages.

Looks, specifically, act as a window into a kid's personal world. The wide grin of a pleased youngster, the wrinkled forehead of one wrestling with disarray, or the downturned lips flagging trouble — all embody the subtleties of profound articulation. Guardians, receptive to these facial signals, can answer with compassion, offering backing or confirmation in light of the youngster's personal state.

Non-verbal communication, one more element of nonverbal correspondence, enhances the quiet language kids use to articulate their thoughts. The drooped shoulders of a crippled kid, the enlivened tokens of an energized narrator, or the squirming of one encountering apprehension — all impart feelings, solace levels, and commitment to a given second.

Motions, while frequently unpretentious, assume a urgent part in conveying significance inside the nonverbal domain. A youngster's energetic wave, a consoling pat on a companion's shoulder, or the energized pointing towards an object of interest all add to the wealth of nonverbal correspondence. These signals, however at times ignored, give important experiences into a kid's expectations, inclinations, and social collaborations.

Eye to eye connection, thought about a strong nonverbal sign, lays out an association among people and mirrors the degree of commitment and mindfulness. A few youngsters may normally keep in touch, flagging certainty and receptiveness in correspondence. Others, notwithstanding, may find supported eye to eye connection testing, showing timidity, social nervousness, or social varieties in correspondence standards.

Understanding and deciphering these nonverbal prompts requires a nuanced approach that thinks about individual contrasts and context oriented factors. Guardians and teachers, by adjusting themselves to the quiet language of nonverbal correspondence, can cultivate conditions that advance capacity to appreciate individuals on a profound level, viable social connections, and a more profound comprehension of every youngster's interesting articulation.

The domain of play fills in as a dynamic and multi-layered field for the statement of kids' correspondence styles. Play, a long way from being simple entertainment, is an imperative medium through which youngsters investigate their inventiveness, social elements, and profound encounters. The language expressed through play envelops a different scope of signs that frequently slip by everyone's notice without cautious perception.

Innovative play, described by the making of situations, jobs, and accounts, permits kids to externalize their considerations and sentiments. The elements inside these play situations give looks into's how kids might interpret social jobs, power elements, and ways of dealing with hardship or stress. A perceptive guardian might observe disregarded prompts in a youngster who reliably depicts a sustaining job, maybe mirroring a requirement for consolation or a craving for providing care.

Children decisions inside play — whether it be the choice of toys, the subjects they investigate, or the characters they epitomize — all add to the quiet account of their inward universes. A kid who floats towards development toys might be communicating an interest in spatial connections and critical thinking. Another who participates in dream play including superheroes might be handling subjects of strength, equity, and individual organization.

Changes in play examples can likewise act as signs of hidden feelings or encounters. A kid who, after a problematic occasion, takes part in play that mirrors components of the experience might be involving play for the purpose of handling and figuring out the occasion. Perceiving these unpretentious changes in play conduct permits guardians and teachers to offer designated help, recognizing and approving the kid's personal reactions.

Social cooperations inside play further enlighten the novel correspondence styles of kids. Peer connections, coordinated effort, compromise, and the exchange of jobs inside play situations all add to the quiet language spoken by kids. An ignored signal in a kid's hesitance to take part in bunch play might demonstrate social uneasiness or a requirement for a more steady prologue to social connections.

Noticing play elements additionally gives experiences into correspondence styles inside connections. A youngster who effectively works together, shares thoughts, and takes part in complementary play is probable showing an open style that values collaboration and association.

Conversely, a youngster who lean towards free play or displays initiative characteristics inside a gathering might be communicating a requirement for independence or an inclination for taking on influential positions.

Understanding the special correspondence styles inside play includes establishing conditions that energize different methods of articulation. Guardians and teachers, by esteeming the extravagance of play-based correspondence, can uphold kids in creating interactive abilities, the capacity to understand people on a profound level, and a feeling of organization inside their connections.

The impact of outer elements on kids' correspondence styles acquaints one more layer with the mind boggling elements of young life articulation. Innovation, with its unavoidable presence in contemporary society, shapes the correspondence styles of youngsters in manners that request cautious thought.

Advanced correspondence, whether through gadgets, web-based entertainment, or virtual stages, acquaints new aspects with youngsters' appearance. Disregarded signals in a youngster's commitment with innovation might appear as changes in screen time conduct, inclinations for explicit computerized exercises, or close to home reactions to online cooperations. A youngster who presentations indications of pain during or after web-based communications might be flagging a requirement for help in exploring the computerized scene.

Understanding the quiet language of innovation includes defining solid limits for screen time as well as participating in open discussions that assist youngsters with articulating their encounters, inclinations, and worries in the advanced domain. Perceiving the disregarded signs inside the advanced scene enables guardians and teachers to direct youngsters in developing dependable and positive computerized citizenship.

Parental impact, profoundly implanted in the texture of experience growing up, fundamentally shapes the correspondence styles of youngsters. The family climate, portrayed via providing care styles, correspondence designs, and the nature of connections, significantly impacts how kids communicate their thoughts and explore relational associations.

Ignored prompts inside relational peculiarities might appear as varieties in correspondence styles, profound articulations, or social reactions. A kid who shows prompts of trouble or withdrawal during snapshots of familial clash might be flagging the profound effect of parental communications. Perceiving these signs prompts parental figures to encourage a climate that focuses on open correspondence, compromise, and close to home prosperity inside the nuclear family.

Parental association and correspondence styles add to the quiet language spoken by kids. A neglected prompt in a youngster's hesitance to share encounters or examine feelings might show a requirement for a more open and steady correspondence channel inside the family. Setting out open doors for significant discussions, undivided attention, and common comprehension empowers guardians to disentangle the quiet language of their kids and answer in a way that sustains close to home prosperity.

Instructive settings, enveloping the school climate and the elements of learning, further shape the correspondence styles of youngsters. Neglected signals inside instructive settings might appear as changes in scholarly execution, commitment levels, or articulations of dissatisfaction or fatigue.

Understanding these prompts requires a comprehensive methodology that considers the different learning styles, inclinations, and individual necessities of every kid. A perceptive teacher might observe ignored signals a scholarly in a youngster, regardless of scholarly capacities, shows withdrawal or social difficulties in the homeroom.

Perceiving these signals prompts instructors to embrace techniques that take care of different learning modalities, encouraging a comprehensive climate that esteems every youngster's novel assets.

The quiet language of kids inside instructive settings is additionally obvious in their reactions to appraisals and assessments. Ignored prompts connected with test uneasiness, execution pressure, or the effect of state sanctioned testing might appear as changes in conduct, close to home pain, or a decrease in scholastic inspiration. Perceiving these signs prompts teachers to investigate elective appraisal techniques, cultivating a climate that values comprehensive learning and recognizes the different qualities of every youngster.

Neurodiversity acquaints one more layer with the quiet language spoken by youngsters, enveloping varieties in mental working, correspondence styles, and tangible encounters. Ignored signs inside the domain of neurodiversity might appear as varieties in tangible awarenesses, correspondence styles, or the statement of one of a kind qualities and difficulties.

Understanding and embracing the quiet language of neurodivergent youngsters requires a guarantee to inclusivity, compassion, and perceiving the worth of different approaches to encountering and communicating oneself. A kid determined to have chemical imbalance range jumble (ASD), for instance, may display signals like an inclination for schedule, aversion to tangible improvements, or extraordinary types of correspondence. Perceiving and obliging these signals permits guardians and instructors to establish conditions that honor the uniqueness of neurodivergent youngsters, encouraging a feeling of consideration and understanding.

Social impacts, profoundly imbued in the quiet language of youngsters, add to varieties in correspondence styles, articulations of character, and the forming of perspectives. Neglected signs inside social settings might appear as varieties in play inclinations, ways to deal with social cooperations, or articulations of personality that reflect social qualities.

Understanding these signals requires social skill, a receptiveness to different viewpoints, and a pledge to establishing conditions that regard and celebrate social variety. A youngster from a multicultural foundation, for example, may show signs, for example, an inclination for specific social exercises, varieties in correspondence styles, or articulations of character that mirror their social legacy. Perceiving and answering these prompts inside a socially skilled system permits teachers and parental figures to establish comprehensive conditions that hug and praise the variety of social impacts.

Orientation elements, profoundly imbued in cultural accounts, add to the quiet language spoken by kids as they explore the intricacies of orientation character and articulation. Disregarded signs inside gendered settings might appear as varieties in play inclinations, articulations of orientation jobs, or signs of distress with cultural assumptions.

Understanding the quiet language of orientation requires a familiarity with the effect of cultural standards and generalizations, and a guarantee to establishing conditions that enable kids to communicate their distinction past prohibitive orientation standards. A youngster impacted by cultural assumptions might show prompts like adherence to customary orientation jobs, articulations of orientation dysphoria, or uneasiness with certain gendered exercises. Perceiving and testing these gendered prompts permits parental figures and teachers to establish conditions that embrace orientation variety, challenge generalizations, and insist every youngster's novel character.

The diversity of ignored prompts envelops the more extensive sociocultural setting that shapes the stories of young life. Culture, with its mind boggling woven artwork of standards, values, and assumptions, impacts how kids communicate their thoughts, explore connections, and see the world. Disregarded prompts inside social settings might appear as varieties in correspondence styles, ways to deal with discipline, or the accentuation put on individual versus aggregate personality.

Perceiving these social subtleties is fundamental for guardians and teachers, as it permits them to decipher the unpretentious prompts in a way that lines up with the social setting, keeping away from misinterpretations and cultivating a more comprehensive climate. For example, a kid from a culture that values cooperation might display signs like areas of strength for a for bunch exercises or uplifted aversion to social elements. Understanding these social prompts permits grown-ups to offer help that regards and praises different social foundations.

In the investigation of neglected signs, the gendered encounters of youngsters arise as another basic feature. Cultural assumptions and generalizations frequently impact how young men and young ladies put themselves out there, explore connections, and draw in with their environmental elements. Disregarded signals in gendered settings might include the unpretentious support of orientation standards in play, the effect of media depictions on self-discernment, or the nuanced manners by which youngsters explore peer cooperations.

Consider a situation where a young man, impacted by cultural assumptions, stifles his feelings to adjust to customary manly standards. The neglected signs in this present circumstance might incorporate unpretentious articulations of close to home limitation, hesitance to participate in supporting play, or the veiling of weakness. Perceiving and testing these gendered signs permits parental figures and instructors to establish conditions that engage kids to communicate their singularity past prohibitive generalizations.

The multifacetedness of disregarded signs additionally recognizes the job of fundamental elements in molding kids' encounters. Issues like neediness, segregation, and lacking admittance to medical care can appear in the ignored signals of kids — whether it be formative postponements, social difficulties, or profound pain.

Youngster backers and policymakers, by recognizing and tending to these prompts, can pursue making foundational changes that guarantee each kid has the potential chance to flourish in a strong and evenhanded climate.

2.2 Unpacking non-verbal cues and expressions that convey unspoken desires.

Unloading the many-sided universe of non-verbal signs and articulations in kids divulges a significant layer of correspondence that frequently slips through the cracks in the clamoring scene of life as a youngster. Past verbally expressed words, youngsters impart through a rich embroidery of motions, looks, non-verbal communication, and unpretentious subtleties that convey their implicit longings, necessities, and feelings. Digging into the domain of non-verbal correspondence requires a sharp observational eye, a comprehension of individual contrasts, and an appreciation for the quiet language that says a lot in the realm of life as a youngster.

Looks act as a strong material for the implicit longings of kids. The human face is a noteworthy instrument equipped for conveying a range of feelings — from the extravagance of satisfaction to the profundities of distress. A youngster's grin, irresistible and real, may connote the craving for association, endorsement, or the basic delight of the current second.

On the other hand, a wrinkled temple or a downturned mouth might flag neglected requirements, inconvenience, or profound pain.

The eyes, frequently alluded to as the windows to the spirit, assume a significant part in communicating implicit longings. A youngster's look, whether consistent or deflected, conveys volumes about their close to home state and wants. The sparkle of fervor in the eyes might uncover a longing for disclosure and experience, while a look turned internal could connote reflection or examination of implied considerations and wants.

Noticing the non-verbal signs inside the domain of looks requires a nuanced comprehension of individual varieties. A few kids might wear their feelings unmistakably on their countenances, offering clear signs to their longings and necessities. Others might veil their sentiments, requiring a more mindful and compassionate way to deal with observe the unobtrusive articulations that double-cross their implicit longings.

Non-verbal communication, a many-sided dance of development and stance, fills in as one more material for the implicit cravings of kids. The drooped shoulders of a down and out kid might convey a longing for solace, consolation, or understanding. On the other hand, the enlivened developments of an energized youngster might mirror a yearning for investigation, commitment, and the satisfaction of their interests.

Signals, however frequently inconspicuous, give an extraordinary language through which youngsters convey their longings without expressing a word. An arriving at hand might communicate a longing for association or a wish to investigate the world reachable. A grasped clench hand might deceive dissatisfaction or the longing for a feeling of control. Understanding these signals includes deciphering them inside the setting of the kid's uniqueness and the particular conditions that encompass their non-verbal articulations.

Vicinity and contact, fundamental parts of non-verbal correspondence, convey implicit longings for association, security, and friendship. A kid who looks for closeness, whether through inclining in, connecting, or nestling, might be communicating a basic requirement for actual association and solace. On the other hand, a kid who pulls back from contact might be flagging a craving for individual space, independence, or a need to freely explore their feelings.

The elements of play, a focal field for youth articulation, offer a novel focal point through which to unload non-verbal signals and implicit longings. In the realm of play, youngsters externalize their contemplations, wants, and feelings through activities, situations, and collaborations. A kid who floats towards certain toys or subjects might be communicating a craving to investigate explicit interests or adapt to unstated feelings.

Consider the situation of two kids participated in cooperative play. The implicit longing for friendship, shared encounters, and a feeling of having a place becomes clear through their joint exercises, shared chuckling, and common commitment. Essentially, a kid who withdraws into singular play might be imparting a craving for contemplation, free investigation, or a snapshot of calm reflection in the midst of the fiery social cooperations of life as a youngster.

The subtleties inside the elements of play stretch out to implicit longings connected with power, control, and the discussion of social jobs. Noticing a kid who reliably expects a position of authority or coordinates the story in play situations might uncover a longing for office, impact, and a feeling of capability. On the other hand, a youngster who readily takes on supporting jobs or concedes to companions might be communicating a craving for cooperation, congruity, and a common feeling of achievement.

Unloading the non-verbal signals inside play likewise includes perceiving the meaning of changes in play designs. A youngster who, after a difficult encounter, integrates components of that experience into their play might be involving play as a remedial device to handle feelings, express longings for dominance, or look for a feeling of control despite vulnerability. Perceiving these movements requires a nuanced comprehension of the youngster's one of a kind play style and the close to home scenes they explore.

Close to home articulations, a center part of non-verbal correspondence, offer a significant look into the implicit longings of kids.

Feelings, whether communicated through tears of disappointment, chuckling of bliss, or the unpretentious subtleties of looks, convey the interior scene of wants, needs, and encounters. A perceptive parental figure or teacher can recognize the implicit longings inside the profound range of a kid, offering backing and approval because of their close to home articulations.

The language of feelings stretches out past basic classifications like satisfaction, bitterness, or outrage. Youngsters, similar to grown-ups, experience a nuanced cluster of feelings that might be trying to verbally lucid. Implicit longings connected with a requirement for approval, understanding, or a feeling of organization might be installed inside the perplexing interchange of feelings.

Consider a kid who presentations indications of uneasiness — an inclination frequently trying for youngsters to unequivocally communicate. The non-verbal signals related with nervousness, for example, squirming, evasion of eye to eye connection, or changes in conduct, may convey implicit cravings for consolation, solace, and a strong presence. Perceiving and answering these signs includes establishing a climate that recognizes the kid's close to home encounters and offers roads for profound articulation and backing.

Social associations, another field where non-verbal signals are pervasive, uncover the implicit longings of kids inside the setting of connections and associations. A youngster's correspondence style in group environments might reflect cravings for consideration, companionship, or a feeling of having a place. On the other hand, signals of uneasiness, withdrawal, or reluctance might show implicit longings for individual space, independence, or the need to explore social collaborations at their own speed.

Understanding the implicit longings inside friendly collaborations requires a nuanced approach that thinks about individual contrasts in disposition, social inclinations, and social impacts. A few kids may normally float towards social scenes, communicating a craving for shared encounters, coordinated effort, and social association. Others might display prompts of introspection, flagging an inclination for lone exercises, free investigation, or a requirement for snapshots of calm reflection.

The job of innovation in contemporary youth acquaints another aspect with the non-verbal signals that convey implicit cravings. As youngsters draw in with advanced gadgets, screens, and virtual conditions, their appearances inside the computerized domain offer bits of knowledge into wants connected with investigation, imagination, and the requirement for computerized network.

Neglected signals in a youngster's computerized conduct might appear as changes in screen time designs, inclinations for explicit advanced exercises, or profound reactions to online communications.

A kid who shows indications of misery or dissatisfaction during computerized commitment might be flagging neglected longings for direction in exploring the advanced scene or a requirement for help in overseeing advanced cooperations. Perceiving these signs includes adjusting the advantages of computerized investigation with the significance of encouraging capable and positive advanced citizenship.

Parental impact, profoundly imbued in the texture of experience growing up, fundamentally shapes the non-verbal signs and implicit cravings of kids. The family climate, portrayed by correspondence designs, providing care styles, and the nature of connections, significantly impacts how kids articulate their thoughts and explore their cravings inside familial elements.

Disregarded signals inside family cooperations might appear as varieties in non-verbal correspondence styles, changes in conduct, or articulations of profound trouble. A kid who presentations prompts of trouble or withdrawal during snapshots of familial struggle might be flagging neglected longings for close to home security, understanding, or a requirement for consolation in the midst of testing circumstances. Perceiving and answering these signs prompts guardians to encourage a climate that focuses on open correspondence, compromise, and profound prosperity inside the nuclear family.

Parental inclusion and correspondence styles contribute altogether to the quiet language spoken by youngsters. A disregarded sign in a youngster's hesitance to share encounters or examine feelings might demonstrate a longing for a more open and strong correspondence channel inside the family. Setting out open doors for significant discussions, undivided attention, and shared understanding empowers guardians to disentangle the non-verbal signals of their youngsters and answer in a way that sustains close to home prosperity.

Instructive settings, incorporating the school climate and the elements of learning, further shape the non-verbal prompts and implicit longings of kids. Neglected prompts inside instructive settings might appear as changes in scholastic execution, commitment levels, or articulations of disappointment or weariness.

Understanding these prompts requires an all encompassing methodology that considers the different learning styles, inclinations, and individual necessities of every youngster. A perceptive teacher might recognize ignored prompts a scholarly in a youngster, in spite of scholarly capacities, shows withdrawal or conduct difficulties in the study hall. Perceiving these signs prompts teachers to embrace procedures that take care of different learning modalities, cultivating a comprehensive climate that esteems every youngster's special assets.

The quiet language of kids inside instructive settings is likewise obvious in their reactions to appraisals and assessments. Neglected prompts connected with test tension, execution pressure, or the effect of government sanctioned testing might appear as changes in conduct, profound pain, or a decrease in scholastic inspiration.

Perceiving these signals prompts instructors to investigate elective appraisal techniques, cultivating a climate that values all encompassing learning and recognizes the assorted qualities of every youngster.

Neurodiversity, a characteristic part of human variety in mental working, acquaints one more layer with the non-verbal prompts and implicit longings of kids. Neglected prompts inside the domain of neurodiversity might appear as varieties in tactile awarenesses, correspondence styles, or the statement of special qualities and difficulties.

Understanding and embracing the non-verbal language of neurodivergent youngsters requires a promise to inclusivity, sympathy, and perceiving the worth of different approaches to encountering and communicating oneself. A kid determined to have mental imbalance range jumble (ASD), for instance, may display signs like an inclination for schedule, aversion to tangible boosts, or novel types of correspondence. Perceiving and obliging these signs permits parental figures and teachers to establish conditions that honor the distinction of neurodivergent kids, encouraging a feeling of consideration and understanding.

Social impacts, profoundly imbued in the non-verbal language of kids, add to varieties in correspondence styles, articulations of personality, and the forming of perspectives. Disregarded signals inside social settings might appear as varieties in play inclinations, ways to deal with social cooperations, or articulations of character that reflect social qualities.

Understanding these prompts requires social skill, a receptiveness to different viewpoints, and a promise to establishing conditions that regard and celebrate social variety. A youngster from a multicultural foundation, for example, may display signs, for example, an inclination for specific social exercises, varieties in correspondence styles, or articulations of character that mirror their social legacy. Perceiving and answering these signals inside a socially skilled structure permits instructors and guardians to establish comprehensive conditions that hug and praise the variety of social impacts.

Orientation elements, profoundly imbued in cultural stories, add to the non-verbal language spoken by youngsters as they explore the intricacies of orientation character and articulation. Disregarded signs inside gendered settings might appear as varieties in play inclinations, articulations of orientation jobs, or signs of distress with cultural assumptions.

Understanding the non-verbal language of orientation requires a consciousness of the effect of cultural standards and generalizations, and a guarantee to establishing conditions that engage youngsters to communicate their distinction past prohibitive orientation standards. A kid impacted by cultural assumptions might show prompts like adherence to customary orientation jobs, articulations of orientation dysphoria, or distress with certain gendered exercises.

Perceiving and testing these gendered signs permits parental figures and instructors to establish conditions that embrace orientation variety, challenge generalizations, and confirm every youngster's exceptional personality.

The interconnection of ignored signs envelops the more extensive sociocultural setting that shapes the stories of young life. Culture, with its multifaceted woven artwork of standards, values, and assumptions, impacts how youngsters communicate their thoughts, explore connections, and see the world. Disregarded signs inside social settings might appear as varieties in correspondence styles, ways to deal with discipline, or the accentuation put on individual versus aggregate personality.

Perceiving these social subtleties is fundamental for parental figures and teachers, as it permits them to decipher the unpretentious signals in a way that lines up with the social setting, staying away from misinterpretations and cultivating a more comprehensive climate. For example, a youngster from a culture that values community might show signals like areas of strength for a for bunch exercises or elevated aversion to social elements. Understanding these social signals permits grown-ups to offer help that regards and praises assorted social foundations.

In the investigation of neglected signs, the gendered encounters of youngsters arise as another basic feature. Cultural assumptions and generalizations frequently impact how young men and young ladies put themselves out there, explore connections, and draw in with their environmental elements. Neglected prompts in gendered settings might include the unobtrusive support of orientation standards in play, the effect of media depictions on self-discernment, or the nuanced manners by which kids explore peer associations.

Consider a situation where a little fellow, impacted by cultural assumptions, smothers his feelings to adjust to customary manly standards. The ignored signals in this present circumstance might incorporate unpretentious articulations of close to home limitation, hesitance to take part in supporting play, or the veiling of weakness. Perceiving and testing these gendered signals permits guardians and teachers to establish conditions that engage kids to communicate their singularity past prohibitive generalizations.

The diversity of disregarded signals additionally recognizes the job of foundational factors in forming youngsters' encounters. Issues like neediness, separation, and lacking admittance to medical care can appear in the ignored signs of youngsters — whether it be formative deferrals, social difficulties, or close to home misery. Kid backers and policymakers, by recognizing and tending to these prompts, can pursue making foundational changes that guarantee each youngster has the potential chance to flourish in a steady and impartial climate.

2.3 How to interpret the language of play, drawings, and gestures.

Deciphering the language of play, drawings, and signals in kids offers an enrapturing venture into the mind boggling domains of their creative mind, feelings, and implicit articulations. Play, as a dynamic and unconstrained movement, fills in as a window into the internal universe of a kid, giving bits of knowledge into their viewpoints, wants, and the manners in which they get a handle on their encounters. Drawings, a fine art open to even the most youthful youngsters, convey a visual language that frequently imparts parts of their profound scene and discernments. Signals, including a range of developments and articulations, structure a nonverbal language that kids use to convey sentiments, requirements, and expectations. Understanding and deciphering these types of correspondence requires a nuanced approach, embracing the uniqueness of every youngster's demeanor inside the settings of play, drawings, and signals.

Play, in its horde structures, fills in as a material where youngsters externalize their considerations, feelings, and wants. From creative play situations to helpful games, youngsters take part in a different scope of exercises that mirror how they might interpret the world, relational elements, and the intricacies of their inside encounters.

In innovative play, youngsters frequently make situations, take on jobs, and submerge themselves in accounts that mirror their discernments, wants, and concerns. A gathering of youngsters participated in an imagine casual get-together may not just be participating in an eccentric movement but rather could be communicating a longing for social association, brotherhood, and the investigation of social jobs. Likewise, a kid who reliably institutes situations including providing care or safeguarding might be imparting their requirement for a feeling of office, obligation, or a longing for supporting.

Noticing the elements inside play situations permits parental figures and teachers to decipher the language of play, knowing implicit prompts connected with social elements, close to home encounters, and the route of mind boggling subjects. Play turns into a medium through which kids articulate their cravings, fears, and survival techniques, offering significant experiences that may not be as promptly communicated through verbal correspondence.

Helpful play, described by cooperation and shared exercises, gives one more aspect to the language of play. Youngsters participated in building structures, playing tabletop games, or taking part in bunch exercises impart their cravings for association, shared encounters, and the satisfaction of shared objectives. The unobtrusive talks, compromises, and articulations of euphoria or dissatisfaction inside helpful play situations offer a nuanced look into the social elements and implicit cravings of the members.

Besides, play fills in as a device for profound articulation and guideline. A youngster who participates in crude play might be delivering repressed energy, looking for tactile info, or communicating a longing for actual perkiness. Then again, a youngster who withdraws into singular play during snapshots of stress or overpower might be flagging a requirement for self-relieving, thoughtfulness, or a longing for a transitory getaway from outside boosts.

Understanding the language of play includes perceiving the meaning of changes in play designs. An unexpected change in the topics investigated, modifications in the power of play, or varieties in the elements of gathering play can all act as marks of implicit longings and close to home encounters. A kid who, after a difficult occasion, integrates components of that experience into their play might be involving play as a survival strategy, handling feelings, and looking for a feeling of control inside the conjured up universe they build.

Drawings, as a visual and unmistakable type of articulation, give one more road through which youngsters impart their contemplations, feelings, and wants. The demonstration of attracting permits youngsters to externalize their inside world, offering a novel look into their discernments, concerns, and the representative language they utilize to convey meaning.

Youngsters' drawings frequently include a blend of conspicuous components — like individuals, creatures, objects — and emblematic portrayals that hold individual importance. A drawing of a family may not just address individuals in the kid's prompt climate however could likewise convey a craving for association, a feeling of having a place, or impressions of familial elements. Essentially, a kid who more than once draws pictures of a specific creature might be communicating a proclivity for that animal, extending parts of their character, or representing wanted characteristics related with the picked creature.

Deciphering youngsters' drawings requires a context oriented understanding that goes past a superficial investigation of the visual components. The varieties picked, the size and position of figures, and the general arrangement add to the visual language that conveys implicit longings and feelings. A drawing overwhelmed by dynamic tones might flag extravagance, bliss, or a longing for consideration, while quieted tones could convey a more thoughtful or pensive temperament.

The emblematic components inside drawings offer rich experiences into the youngster's inner world. A repetitive topic of disengagement, portrayed through the situation of figures a ways off or inside isolated spaces, may demonstrate sensations of depression, a longing for individual space, or difficulties in exploring social collaborations. On the other hand, drawings highlighting closeness, shared spaces, and interconnecting components might convey a craving for association, cooperation, and a feeling of solidarity.

Besides, changes in drawing topics after some time give a unique story of a youngster's developing cravings, encounters, and profound scene. A youngster who, after a huge life altering situation, shifts from attracting scenes of disorder to pictures of request and association might be communicating a longing for soundness, control, and a feeling of rationality despite change. Perceiving these movements requires an adjusted and sympathetic methodology that esteems the kid's visual language as a legitimate and significant type of articulation.

Signals, incorporating many developments and articulations, structure a nonverbal language that youngsters instinctually use to convey their sentiments, necessities, and goals. From straightforward hand developments to looks, signals offer a quick and direct means through which youngsters convey in different settings.

Looks, as a subset of signals, assume a focal part in conveying implicit cravings and feelings. A youngster's grin might communicate satisfaction, happiness, or a craving for positive cooperation. On the other hand, a wrinkled temple, a frown, or tears might mean disappointment, inconvenience, or the requirement for help. Parental figures and teachers receptive to these looks can answer with sympathy, offering solace, approval, or help in view of the kid's personal state.

Hand signals, one more basic part of nonverbal correspondence, add to the language of motions. A kid's energetic wave might communicate a longing for association, hello, or affirmation. Pointing towards an object of interest imparts a wish to share an encounter, draw consideration, or express interest. On the other hand, signals, for example, crossing arms, staying away from eye to eye connection, or pulling out into oneself might show sensations of distress, opposition, or a requirement for individual space.

Noticing a youngster's motions inside friendly collaborations gives significant bits of knowledge into their implicit longings connected with association, commitment, and solace. A youngster who with certainty participates in enlivened motions, keeps in touch, and takes part effectively in discussions might be communicating a longing for social association, acknowledgment, and shared commitment. Conversely, a youngster who shows saved motions, evades direct eye to eye connection, or presentations faltering in friendly collaborations might be flagging a requirement for a more progressive or strong way to deal with social commitment.

The language of signals reaches out past looks and hand developments to envelop the whole body. Non-verbal communication, portrayed by stance, developments, and generally speaking actual disposition, conveys implicit longings connected with solace, certainty, and commitment. A youngster who stands tall, moves with energy, and participates in sweeping signals might be communicating a craving for investigation, organization, and a feeling of imperativeness. On the other hand, a youngster who takes on a more held act, maintains a strategic distance from eye to eye connection, or shows tense developments might be flagging sensations of uneasiness, timidity, or a requirement for a more strong and grasping methodology.

Understanding signals likewise includes perceiving the social subtleties that impact nonverbal correspondence. Various societies might credit differed implications to motions, looks, and non-verbal communication. A motion that connotes confirmation in one social setting might pass on an alternate message in another. Parental figures and teachers drawing in with kids from different social foundations benefit from social capability, permitting them to decipher signals inside a structure that regards and values the social variety of the kid.

Deciphering the language of play, drawings, and signals includes developing an adjusted and sympathetic methodology that praises the uniqueness of every youngster's appearance. It requires a readiness to go past superficial perceptions, digging into the layers of imagery, setting, and individual varieties that add to the rich embroidery of correspondence in youth.

Also, the translation of these types of correspondence requires an affirmation of the unique idea of experience growing up. Youngsters' looks advance, answering formative achievements, educational encounters, and the steadily changing scenes of their feelings. Guardians and teachers participated in the interpretative excursion should stay open to continuous perceptions, perceiving that the language of play, drawings, and signals fills in as a liquid and developing story of a youngster's inward world.

Chapter 3

The Mask of Normalcy

The Veil of Business as usual: Disclosing the Mind boggling Real factors Behind Congruity

In the complicated dance of cultural assumptions and individual personality, the idea of the "Veil of Business as usual" arises as a significant investigation into the intricacies of congruity and the secret battles that people frequently wrestle with underneath the facade of cultural assumptions. The veil, emblematic of the veneer introduced to the world, disguises the subtleties of one's actual self, individual difficulties, and the struggles under the surface that emerge from the tensions to adjust. This figurative veil, wore by people in different parts of life, envelops cultural standards, social assumptions, and the craving for acknowledgment, bringing up issues about legitimacy, mental prosperity, and the quest for a veritable identity.

At its center, the Cover of Predictability mirrors the inborn strain between cultural assumptions and the singular journey for credibility. Society, with its unpredictable trap of standards, values, and assumptions, frequently forces a bunch of guidelines that people are supposed with comply to. These norms, whether relating to appearance, conduct, or life decisions, make an outer structure that impacts how people introduce themselves to the world. The strain to adjust to these standards can prompt the reception of a cover — a painstakingly created persona that lines up with cultural assumptions while hiding the intricacies that lie underneath the surface.

The elements of the Veil of Predictability are especially articulated in the domain of psychological well-being. People wrestling with psychological wellness difficulties might feel a sense of urgency to wear a veil to hide their battles, dreading the disgrace, judgment, or misconception that can go with revelation. The strain to show up "typical" increases as cultural discernments frequently slander psychological well-being conditions, adding to an environment where people might decide to conceal their genuine encounters behind an exterior of prosperity.

The work environment turns into a huge field where the Veil of Business as usual is regularly worn. Proficient conditions frequently stress attributes like certainty, ability, and strength, making an assumption for representatives to extend a picture of accomplishment and unfaltering capacity. The apprehension about being seen as powerless or unable can lead people to hide individual difficulties, stressors, or snapshots of self-uncertainty behind the Veil of Predictability. The work environment, while advancing a culture of accomplishment, can unintentionally add to a feeling of separation and disengagement as people wrestle with their bona fide selves underneath the exterior.

Social and cultural assumptions further shape the forms of the Veil of Predictability. The strain to adjust to explicit orientation jobs, social standards, or cultural beliefs of accomplishment adds layers to the intricacy of the veil. People might wind up exploring a sensitive harmony between sticking to outside assumptions and embracing their interesting characters. This subtle conflict can prompt a divided identity, with the veil turning into a component for exploring the intricacies of cultural standards while protecting a similarity to singularity.

Besides, the coming of online entertainment acquaints another aspect with the Veil of Business as usual. The organized stories and painstakingly created pictures introduced on friendly stages frequently mirror a romanticized form of life, adding to a culture of examination and flawlessness. People might feel a sense of urgency to adjust to cultural guidelines of magnificence, achievement, or bliss, sustaining the pattern of wearing a veil to project a picture that lines up with winning standards. The hole between organized web-based personas and the bona fide lived encounters of people highlights the unavoidable impact of the Veil of Business as usual in the advanced age.

The quest for acknowledgment and having a place enhances the force of the Veil of Business as usual. People, innately friendly animals, need association and endorsement from their companions. The anxiety toward dismissal or segregation can drive people to wear a cover that lines up with winning standards, regardless of whether it implies stifling parts of their actual selves. The journey for social acknowledgment turns into a main impetus, molding ways of behaving, decisions, and self-show to fit inside the boundaries of cultural assumptions.

The Veil of Business as usual broadens its venture into the domain of connections, where people might explore the intricacies of special interactions by projecting a picture that lines up with apparent standards of a "typical" accomplice, companion, or relative. The apprehension about judgment, dismissal, or struggle can lead people to stifle parts of their credible selves, adding to a feeling of separation inside connections. The conundrum arises as the longing for veritable association conflicts with the propensity to wear a veil for congruity or acknowledgment.

Kids, since early on, are acquainted with the idea of cultural standards and assumptions. The school system, familial impacts, and friend elements all add to the early development of the Cover of Predictability. Kids might figure out how to hide parts of their character or exceptional attributes to line up with the assumptions for power figures or companions. The early reception of the veil establishes the groundwork for an example of congruity that might continue into adulthood, influencing self-revelation and credible articulation.

Disentangling the layers of the Cover of Predictability requires an excursion internal, encouraging mindfulness, and embracing weakness. The initial step includes recognizing the presence of the cover and perceiving its effect on individual prosperity. Breaking liberated from the limitations of cultural assumptions requires a gallant investigation of one's genuine self, embracing the uniqueness that lies past the cover.

Besides, encouraging a culture of sympathy and understanding is fundamental in destroying the Veil of Business as usual. Society, work environments, instructive organizations, and networks assume vital parts in establishing conditions that esteem validness, variety, and the acknowledgment of individual contrasts. Drives that destigmatize psychological wellness, challenge unbending orientation standards, and celebrate different articulations of personality add to a culture where people feel enabled to shed the cover and embrace their actual selves.

With regards to emotional wellness, advancing open discussions and giving strong assets assists people with feeling seen and heard. Psychological wellness drives that focus on destigmatization, openness to assets, and a culture of understanding make spaces where people can explore their emotional well-being ventures really. The affirmation of psychological wellness as a continuum of encounters, as opposed to a twofold of health or sickness, adds to a culture that dismisses the requirement for a cover in the domain of mental prosperity.

Work environments, as critical forces to be reckoned with of individual prosperity, can add to destroying the Cover of Business as usual by encouraging societies of straightforwardness, sympathy, and balance between fun and serious activities. Perceiving and obliging the different necessities of representatives, giving emotional well-being assets, and testing the assumption for steady efficiency add to a work environment culture that values people past their expert veneers.

Social moves that challenge conventional orientation standards and celebrate assorted articulations of character make ready for destroying the Cover of Predictability with regards to orientation assumptions. Embracing the smoothness of orientation personality, cultivating inclusivity, and dismissing generalizations add to a general public where people can communicate their orientation character truly, without the requirement for an adjusting cover.

In the computerized age, advancing advanced education and empowering careful web-based entertainment use mitigates the effect of the arranged internet based personas adding to the Veil of Business as usual. Instructing people, particularly the more youthful age, about the expected entanglements of correlation, the worth of validness, and the nuanced reality behind internet based introductions adds to a better computerized culture.

In connections, cultivating open correspondence, compassion, and acknowledgment makes spaces where people have a good sense of reassurance enough to eliminate their covers. Developing a climate where weakness is commended and contrasts are embraced adds to the improvement of bona fide associations.

3.1 Examining the façade of apparent normalcy that conceals deeper needs.

Inspecting the Façade of Obvious Predictability: Disentangling Further Requirements

In the embroidery of human life, the façade of evident business as usual frequently fills in as a very much created cover, hiding the complicated layers of more profound necessities, wants, and weaknesses that people explore underneath the surface. The idea of clear predictability proposes a superficial adjustment to cultural assumptions, introducing an outward picture that lines up with winning standards. Notwithstanding, underneath this facade lies a mind boggling transaction of profound, mental, and existential necessities that shape the credible pith of a person. This investigation digs into the assessment of obvious predictability, disclosing the multi-layered aspects that highlight the further necessities people wrestle with chasing figuring out, association, and satisfaction.

At its pith, clear business as usual appears as a cultural develop, forming the assumptions and guidelines people feel a sense of urgency to meet. The strain to extend a picture of business as usual is profoundly imbued in cultural accounts, impacting different features of life, including connections, workplaces, instructive foundations, and social assumptions. The craving to fit inside these standards frequently drives people to develop a façade that lines up with outer assumptions, making a superficial depiction of predictability that gives a false representation of the complicated inward scenes they explore.

In the domain of psychological wellness, the façade of clear business as usual turns out to be especially articulated. Emotional wellness conditions, frequently trashed and misconstrued, brief people to wear a cover that conceals the conflicts under the surface they face.

The apprehension about judgment, dismissal, or disengagement can drive people to keep a presentation of business as usual, even as they wrestle with significant close to home and mental difficulties underneath the surface. This inner turmoil between the requirement for genuineness and the cultural strain to adjust adds to the inescapable pervasiveness of stowed away emotional wellness battles.

The working environment, as a microcosm of cultural assumptions, turns into a huge field where the façade of clear business as usual is regularly taken on. Proficient conditions underline characteristics like skill, strength, and certainty, making an assumption for representatives to extend a picture of capacity and achievement. The apprehension about being seen as helpless or unfit can lead people to hide individual difficulties, stressors, or snapshots of self-uncertainty behind the façade of evident business as usual. The work environment, while advancing a culture of accomplishment, can unintentionally add to a feeling of disengagement and separation as people wrestle with their valid selves underneath the surface.

Besides, connections, whether familial, heartfelt, or non-romantic, are frequently impacted by the façade of clear predictability. The longing for acknowledgment, having a place, and association prompts people to project a picture that lines up with apparent goals of a "typical" accomplice, companion, or relative. The feeling of dread toward judgment or dismissal might lead people to disguise parts of their actual selves, making a disharmony between the projected predictability and the legitimate requirements for grasping, acknowledgment, and veritable association inside connections.

Instructive establishments, imbued in cultural standards, likewise add to the development of the façade of evident business as usual. Understudies, since early on, may feel a sense of urgency to adjust to assumptions connected with scholarly accomplishment, conduct, and social cooperations. The strain to fit inside predefined standards can prompt the concealment of independence, preventing the true articulation of one of a kind requirements, interests, and difficulties. The façade of evident predictability in instructive settings might cloud the more deeply needs for customized learning draws near, psychological wellness support, and an acknowledgment of different learning styles.

Social and cultural assumptions further shape the façade of clear predictability. The strain to adjust to explicit orientation jobs, social standards, or cultural goals of accomplishment adds layers to the intricacy of the veil. People might end up exploring a fragile harmony between sticking to outer assumptions and embracing their interesting personalities. This inner turmoil can prompt a divided identity, with the façade turning into a system for exploring the intricacies of cultural standards while protecting a similarity to uniqueness.

The quest for material achievement and cultural endorsement enhances the force of the façade of evident business as usual. The outside markers of progress — monetary soundness, vocation accomplishments, and societal position — frequently become measurements against which people measure their own value and predictability. The tireless quest for these outer markers can lead people to focus on the façade of achievement over the genuine investigation of their more profound requirements for reason, significance, and satisfaction.

Besides, the effect of virtual entertainment in the contemporary scene acquaints another aspect with the façade of evident business as usual. The organized stories and painstakingly created pictures introduced on friendly stages add to a culture of examination and flawlessness. People might feel a sense of urgency to adjust to cultural guidelines of magnificence, achievement, or bliss, propagating the pattern of projecting a picture that lines up with winning standards. The hole between arranged web-based personas and the legitimate lived encounters of people highlights the unavoidable impact of the façade of clear predictability in the computerized age.

Disentangling the more profound necessities that lie underneath the façade of evident business as usual requires a nuanced comprehension of the human experience. The initial step includes recognizing the presence of the façade and perceiving its effect on individual prosperity. The inner turmoil between the projected business as usual and the genuine requirements for association, understanding, and satisfaction requires an excursion internal — a gutsy investigation of one's actual self past cultural assumptions.

The assessment of emotional wellness inside the setting of the façade of obvious business as usual requests a change in perspective in cultural mentalities. Destigmatizing emotional wellness conditions, cultivating open discussions, and establishing strong conditions add to an environment where people feel enabled to shed the façade and look for help unafraid of judgment. Emotional wellness drives that focus on anticipation, early mediation, and open assets address the further necessities people wrestle with in their inward scenes.

Working environments, as powerful spaces, assume a significant part in destroying the façade of evident predictability. Developing a culture of straightforwardness, sympathy, and mental prosperity advances conditions where workers feel seen, heard, and upheld. Perceiving and obliging the different necessities of people, giving assets to balance between serious and fun activities, and testing the assumption for steady efficiency add to working environments that esteem people past their expert façades.

In connections, cultivating open correspondence, compassion, and acknowledgment makes spaces where people have a good sense of reassurance enough to eliminate the façade. Developing a climate where weakness is commended and contrasts are embraced adds to the improvement of genuine associations. Perceiving that everybody conveys further requirements for grasping, approval, and association highlights the significance of genuine correspondence in connections.

Instructive establishments, as developmental spaces, can add to destroying the façade of clear business as usual by embracing variety in learning styles, giving psychological wellness assets, and perceiving the uniqueness of understudies. Establishing conditions where understudies feel urged to communicate their real selves cultivates a culture that esteems the novel requirements, interests, and difficulties of every student.

Social moves that challenge customary orientation standards and celebrate assorted articulations of character prepare for destroying the façade of evident business as usual with regards to cultural assumptions. Embracing the smoothness of orientation character, encouraging inclusivity, and dismissing generalizations add to a general public where people can communicate their personality really, without the requirement for an adjusting façade.

In the computerized age, advancing advanced education and empowering careful virtual entertainment use mitigates the effect of the organized web-based personas adding to the façade of obvious business as usual. Teaching people, particularly the more youthful age, about the possible traps of correlation, the worth of credibility, and the nuanced reality behind web-based introductions adds to a better computerized culture.

The quest for material achievement, frequently interweaved with cultural endorsement, can be reexamined to line up with valid individual requirements. Perceiving that genuine satisfaction emerges from a more profound feeling of direction, significant associations, and self-improvement moves the concentration from outside markers of progress to inward wellsprings of happiness. Empowering people to investigate and focus on their novel requirements adds to a culture that values realness over the shallow façade of obvious predictability.

3.2 The impact of societal expectations and parental assumptions on understanding a child's true desires.

The Effect of Cultural Assumptions and Parental Suppositions on Figuring out a Kid's Actual Longings: Exploring the Intricate Elements of Life as a youngster Articulation

Youth, with its unlimited interest and inventive investigation, is an extraordinary phase of human improvement where understanding a kid's actual cravings requires a nuanced approach. Be that as it may, the effect of cultural assumptions and parental presumptions stirs up misgivings about the scene of life as a youngster articulation. The focal point through which society sees youth, combined with parental biases, can impact the translation of a youngster's ways of behaving, inclinations, and desires. This investigation dives into the complicated elements that shape the comprehension of a youngster's actual cravings, looking at the job of cultural assumptions and parental presumptions in exploring the complex domain of experience growing up articulation.

Cultural assumptions, frequently profoundly imbued in social stories, develop a system through which youth is seen and deciphered. The shared mindset of society shapes winning standards in regards to orientation jobs, scholastic accomplishment, social ways of behaving, and different parts of young life advancement. These assumptions, while giving a similarity to structure, can coincidentally restrict the expansiveness of understanding with regards to knowing a kid's actual cravings.

Orientation standards, for example, assume a critical part in molding cultural assumptions encompassing youth articulation. Customary orientation generalizations endorse explicit ways of behaving, interests, and jobs for young men and young ladies. The cultural content directs that young men ought to be keen on vehicles, sports, and confident play, while young ladies are supposed to float towards dolls, supporting exercises, and calm play. These assumptions make a system that might eclipse a youngster's real advantages and tendencies, as their inclinations are sifted from the perspective of cultural orientation standards.

As a result, a kid who communicates an interest in customarily female exercises might confront cultural obstruction or parental concern. Essentially, a young lady intensely for sports might experience inconspicuous or obvious debilitation. The effect of these cultural assumptions stretches out past the prompt reaction to a youngster's decisions, impacting their self-discernment and forming how they might interpret what is considered OK or proper.

Scholarly assumptions address one more feature of cultural standards that can influence the comprehension of a kid's actual longings. The accentuation on government sanctioned testing, scholarly accomplishment, and foreordained achievements can eclipse a kid's extraordinary learning style, interests, and speed of improvement. Kids might wind up exploring an instructive scene that focuses on similarity over individualized investigation, possibly prompting a distinction between their legitimate cravings for learning and the assumptions forced by the schooling system.

Besides, cultural assumptions about friendly ways of behaving and relational elements add to the intricacy of figuring out a youngster's actual cravings. The strain to adjust to normal practices, make companions, and display explicit interactive abilities can impact a youngster's conduct in manners that may not line up with their genuine tendencies. A youngster who is normally independent might feel a sense of urgency to embrace outgoing ways of behaving to measure up to cultural assumptions, possibly covering their actual cravings for lone exercises or more profound associations with a limited handful.

The effect of cultural assumptions is interlaced with the focal point through which guardians see and decipher their youngster's ways of behaving.

Parental suspicions, formed by cultural standards, social impacts, and individual encounters, can either upgrade or thwart the comprehension of a youngster's actual cravings. Guardians, notwithstanding their best aims, may unknowingly extend their own assumptions onto their youngsters, affecting how they decipher and answer their kid's demeanors.

Yet again orientation assumptions, assume a significant part in parental suppositions about a youngster's cravings. Guardians may incidentally build up conventional orientation jobs by empowering specific exercises or deterring others in light of cultural standards. The suspicions about what is thought of "typical" for a kid or a young lady can influence the open doors and encounters guardians accommodate their kids, possibly restricting the extent of a kid's investigation and self-disclosure.

Parental goals for scholastic achievement can likewise shape presumptions about a kid's actual longings. The craving for a kid to succeed scholastically, determined by cultural assumptions encompassing accomplishment, may incidentally eclipse the youngster's singular advantages and interests. The strain to measure up to parental assumptions can make a dynamic where a youngster's quest for their actual longings is impacted by the craving to satisfy parental yearnings, possibly prompting a misalignment between outside progress and inner satisfaction.

Besides, the cultural accentuation on extracurricular exercises, organized plans, and a pressed schedule can influence how guardians see and focus on their youngster's cravings. The presumption that a balanced kid is one participated in a huge number of exercises might prompt overscheduling, generally ruling out unstructured play, independent investigation, and the quest for individual interests that may not fit conveniently into the cultural shape of progress.

Exploring the effect of cultural assumptions and parental suppositions on understanding a kid's actual longings requires a cognizant work to encourage a climate of genuineness and open correspondence. Guardians, as essential guardians and powerhouses, assume a vital part in making a space where youngsters feel seen, heard, and figured out past cultural standards and parental assumptions.

Empowering open correspondence includes effectively paying attention to a kid's demeanors, interests, and inclinations without forcing assumptions. Establishing a climate where a kid has a good sense of security to divide their actual cravings requires an equilibrium among offering direction and permitting the space for free investigation. Guardians can assume a urgent part in destroying orientation generalizations by presenting youngsters to a different scope of exercises and empowering them to seek after interests without requirements in view of cultural assumptions.

Also, guardians can cultivate an appreciation for individualized learning styles by perceiving and commending the exceptional qualities and gifts of every kid.

Embracing an all encompassing perspective on training that goes past normalized measurements permits guardians to help their kid's actual cravings for learning and scholarly investigation. This includes recognizing that outcome in schooling envelops a range of capacities, interests, and approaches to drawing in with the world.

Setting out open doors for unstructured play and independent investigation is vital in figuring out a kid's actual longings. The strain to adjust to organized exercises and extracurricular responsibilities might impede a kid's capacity to find and seek after their valid advantages. Permitting time with the expectation of complimentary play, creative exercises, and free revelation cultivates a feeling of independence and self-disclosure, empowering youngsters to communicate their actual cravings in a characteristic and unreasonable way.

Guardians can likewise challenge cultural assumptions by effectively captivating with their youngster's social turn of events. Empowering genuine social collaborations, regarding a youngster's requirement for isolation or more profound associations, and encouraging compassion towards different social articulations add to a's comprehension kid might interpret their actual cravings in the domain of relational connections. By perceiving and approving a youngster's valid social tendencies, guardians assume a key part in advancing certifiable associations in light of common comprehension and regard.

Moreover, the effect of cultural assumptions and parental presumptions on understanding a kid's actual cravings can be relieved through schooling and mindfulness. Guardians benefit from continuous self-reflection, investigating their own inclinations, and testing presumptions that may accidentally impact how they might interpret their youngster. Taking part in discussions with different guardians, teachers, and experts in youngster improvement makes an aggregate mindfulness that challenges cultural standards and cultivates a more comprehensive and bona fide way to deal with youth.

Instructive foundations likewise assume a part in molding cultural assumptions and, thusly, parental presumptions. An educational program that embraces variety, individualized learning, and an all encompassing way to deal with schooling can add to a change in outlook in how kids' longings are seen and sustained. Instructors, furnished with a comprehension of the effect of cultural assumptions, can effectively make progress toward establishing conditions that esteem every youngster's novel articulation and investigation of their actual longings.

3.3 Strategies for peeling back the layers to reveal authentic emotions.

Procedures for Stripping Back the Layers to Uncover Legitimate Feelings: Sustaining Veritable Articulation in People

In the mind boggling embroidery of human feelings, the capacity to strip back the layers and uncover real sentiments is a nuanced expertise that encourages certified association and mindfulness. Divulging the genuine feelings that lie underneath the surface requires a fragile comprehension of both oneself as well as other people. This investigation dives into systems pointed toward stripping back these layers, supporting a climate where people can really communicate their feelings, cultivating further associations and advancing close to home prosperity.

Self-reflection fills in as a basic technique for stripping back the layers of one's feelings. Taking deliberate minutes for contemplation permits people to investigate the unpredictable scene of their sentiments, recognize basic feelings, and observe the elements affecting their profound reactions. This interaction includes developing care, making a space for mindfulness, and recognizing the intricacy of feelings without judgment.

Journaling ends up being a significant device in the excursion of self-reflection. Through the demonstration of composing, people can verbalize their contemplations and feelings, acquiring lucidity and understanding into their inward world. Journaling gives a confidential space to communicate real sentiments without outer impact, filling in as an extension between the inside close to home scene and outside understanding. The composed word turns into a mirror that mirrors the profundity and subtleties of one's feelings, working with the most common way of stripping back the layers.

Moreover, care rehearses, like reflection and profound breathing activities, add to the stripping back of close to home layers. These practices make a psychological space that urges people to notice their feelings without quick responses or decisions. Care permits people to foster an elevated consciousness of their close to home encounters, making ready for a more significant comprehension of true sentiments.

In relational connections, dynamic and sympathetic listening arises as a strong system for stripping back the layers of others' feelings. Veritable listening includes more than hearing words; it requires a receptiveness to understanding the feelings conveyed, both verbally and non-verbally. By making a place of refuge where people feel appreciated and approved, undivided attention cultivates a climate helpful for bona fide profound articulation.

The specialty of posing unassuming inquiries assumes a correlative part in working with real profound articulation. Empowering people to dig further into their sentiments by suggesting conversation starters that welcome reflection and self-revelation opens roads for authentic correspondence. By communicating a genuine interest in understanding someone else's personal scene, people are bound to strip back layers and offer true feelings.

Making a culture of weakness and transparency inside connections builds up the techniques for uncovering valid feelings. At the point when people have a good sense of safety in communicating their actual sentiments unafraid of judgment or repercussions, they are more disposed to strip back the layers and offer the profundity of their profound encounters. Developing trust and close to home wellbeing becomes vital in encouraging a climate where genuineness can flourish.

Imaginative and inventive articulations give an elective road to uncovering genuine feelings. Whether through visual expressions, music, dance, or other imaginative outlets, people can channel their feelings into expressive structures. These mediums act as a vehicle for making an interpretation of mind boggling sentiments into unmistakable articulations that might be trying to pass on through words alone. Taking part in imaginative undertakings turns into a system for stripping back close to home layers and offering an exceptional look into one's inward world.

Remedial intercessions, like advising and psychotherapy, offer organized ways to deal with stripping back profound layers. Prepared experts guide people through the course of self-investigation, giving a steady space to revealing and grasping credible feelings. Treatment can be especially viable in tending to well established feelings, irritating issues, and imbued examples of profound articulation that might be impeding genuine self-revelation.

Developing capacity to understand individuals on a profound level arises as an all encompassing procedure for stripping back layers and cultivating genuine close to home articulation. The ability to appreciate individuals on a profound level includes perceiving, understanding, and dealing with one's own feelings, as well as being sensitive to the feelings of others. By sharpening the capacity to appreciate anyone on a profound level, people foster the abilities important to explore the unpredictable layers of feelings, recognize credible sentiments, and convey them really.

Building a jargon for feelings is a major part of creating the capacity to understand individuals on a profound level. Frequently, people might battle to express their sentiments because of a restricted close to home jargon. Teaching oneself about the assorted scope of feelings and figuring out how to distinguish and communicate nuanced sentiments improves the limit with regards to credible close to home correspondence. This cycle enables people to strip back layers with accuracy and clearness.

In the domain of relational elements, laying out clear limits turns into an essential system for establishing a climate helpful for bona fide profound articulation. Solid limits give people a feeling of safety and independence, permitting them to share their feelings without the feeling of dread toward interruption or infringement. Regarding and conveying limits adds to a culture that values individual organization and cultivates certifiable close to home revelation.

Mental social strategies offer commonsense apparatuses for stripping back layers by tending to figured examples and conviction frameworks that might impact close to home articulation. By inspecting and testing mutilated or restricting convictions, people can uncover the center feelings that might be darkened by mental twists. Mental conduct methodologies engage people to reshape their points of view, working with a more legitimate articulation of feelings.

Intelligent practices, like directed self-reflection or contemplative activities, give organized systems to stripping back close to home layers. These practices urge people to investigate explicit parts of their feelings, for example, distinguishing triggers, figuring out examples of reaction, and uncovering well established sentiments. Organized reflection goes about as a conscious and purposeful methodology for stripping back layers and acquiring understanding into legitimate profound encounters.

Care based mediations, like persuasive conduct treatment (DBT) and care based pressure decrease (MBSR), incorporate care rehearses with remedial ways to deal with upgrade profound mindfulness and guideline. These intercessions offer techniques for remaining present with feelings, noticing them without judgment, and developing a non-receptive mindfulness. Care turns into an amazing asset for stripping back profound layers and embracing the extravagance of true close to home encounters.

Social capability assumes a fundamental part in the methodologies for stripping back close to home layers, perceiving that social foundations impact the articulation and translation of feelings. People from different social settings might have unmistakable approaches to conveying feelings, and social responsiveness is fundamental for understanding and regarding these varieties. Techniques that recognize and integrate social subtleties add to a comprehensive way to deal with genuine profound articulation.

Relational peculiarities essentially influence the techniques for stripping back profound layers, especially with regards to adolescence and childhood. Establishing an open and informative family climate permits kids to foster a solid relationship with their feelings since the beginning. Guardians who model bona fide close to home articulation and urge their youngsters to talk about their thoughts add to the advancement of genuinely savvy people who are proficient at stripping back layers.

The combination of innovation and advanced stages presents new open doors for uncovering true feelings. Online stages, support gatherings, and virtual networks offer spaces where people might feel more open to communicating their feelings. The secrecy given by computerized correspondence can be an impetus for stripping back layers, as people might find it more straightforward to share weak parts of their feelings without the quick presence of others.

Proceeding with the investigation of techniques for stripping back layers to uncover legitimate feelings includes a more profound assessment of explicit intercessions and practices that add to cultivating real close to home articulation. The intricacy of human feelings and the different variables that impact their indication require a nuanced and complete way to deal with urge people to divulge their genuine sentiments.

Account Treatment and Narrating:

Story treatment, a type of psychotherapy, gives a stage to people to develop and share their biographies. By portraying their encounters, people can dig into the close to home subtleties of their excursions, disentangling layers of feelings that might be implanted in private stories. This approach works with an intelligent cycle, permitting people to distinguish examples, subjects, and essential minutes that add to their close to home scene. Narrating turns into a method for externalizing feelings as well as acquiring a more profound comprehension of the stories that shape one's personal reactions.

Expressive Expressions Treatment:

Taking part in expressive expressions, like visual expressions, music, dance, or show, fills in as a typified procedure for stripping back profound layers. Human expressions offer a non-verbal road for people to channel and communicate complex feelings that might be trying to verbally lucid. The innovative strategy turns into a type of therapy, permitting people to externalize and investigate their deepest sentiments. Expressive expressions treatment gives a comprehensive way to deal with close to home articulation, taking advantage of the tactile and instinctive parts of human experience.

Connection Informed Approaches:

Understanding the effect of early connection encounters on close to home articulation is critical for stripping back layers. Connection informed approaches in treatment and relational connections perceive the meaning of early guardian connections in molding profound reactions. By investigating and handling connection elements, people can acquire bits of knowledge into how early social encounters impact their present close to home articulations. This approach encourages a humane comprehension of oneself as well as other people, making ready for valid close to home exposure.

Feeling Centered Treatment (EFT):

Feeling centered treatment is a remedial methodology that spotlights on assisting people with turning out to be more mindful of their feelings, figure out their close to home encounters, and express their sentiments in a sound way. Through intercessions intended to get to and investigate feelings, people can strip back layers of close to home protections and find the true center sentiments underneath. EFT underscores the significance of recognizing and approving feelings, making a place of refuge for people to communicate their actual sentiments without judgment.

Careful Development Practices:

Consolidating careful development rehearses, like yoga or jujitsu, into one's normal can be instrumental in stripping back profound layers. These practices consolidate actual development with care, empowering people to be available with their real sensations and feelings. The brain body association developed through careful development permits people to investigate and deliver repressed feelings put away in the body, adding to a more coordinated and credible close to home insight.

Intelligent Discourse and Friend Backing:

Participating in intelligent exchange, either through helpful discussions or companion support gatherings, gives a social space to people to share and ponder their feelings. The intelligent cycle includes undivided attention, compassionate reactions, and shared investigation of feelings. Peer support gatherings, specifically, offer the chance for people to interface with other people who might have comparative encounters, making a strong local area where genuine feelings can be communicated unafraid of judgment.

Injury Informed Approaches:

For people who have encountered injury, injury informed approaches are fundamental for making a setting where true feelings can surface. Injury delicate practices recognize the effect of injury on close to home articulation and focus on security, trust, and strengthening. Establishing an injury informed climate includes perceiving likely triggers, giving decision and independence in the mending system, and encouraging a feeling of organization in exploring one's close to home excursion.

Developing Profound Versatility:

Building close to home flexibility is a proactive procedure for stripping back profound layers and fostering a vigorous ability to explore a scope of sentiments. Profound flexibility includes adjusting to affliction, overseeing pressure, and returning quickly from difficulties. Practices, for example, mental rebuilding, appreciation activities, and positive brain research intercessions add to the advancement of profound versatility. By upgrading one's capacity to adapt to feelings, people become more adroit at stripping back layers and really communicating their sentiments.

Social Capability in Close to home Articulation:

Perceiving and regarding social variety is urgent in systems for uncovering bona fide feelings. Social ability includes understanding how various societies see, express, and explore feelings. Approaches that consolidate social responsiveness guarantee that people from different foundations feel recognized and approved in their exceptional profound articulations. This inclusivity adds to establishing conditions where validness can thrive across social settings.

Diversity in Profound Articulation:

Understanding the multifacetedness of character factors, like race, orientation, sexuality, and financial status, is fundamental in procedures for genuine profound articulation. Multifacetedness perceives that people epitomize numerous layers of personality, and these meeting factors impact their close to home encounters. By recognizing and investigating the intricacy of character, people can strip back layers molded by different meeting parts of their lives, cultivating a more nuanced comprehension of true feelings.

Techniques for stripping back layers to uncover real feelings envelop a different exhibit of helpful modalities, expressive practices, and relational methodologies. The nuanced idea of human feelings requires a customized and complex methodology that thinks about individual contrasts, social settings, and the interconnectedness of close to home encounters. By embracing these procedures, people can leave on an excursion of self-disclosure, encouraging further associations, and developing close to home prosperity.

Chapter 4

The Quiet Cravings

In the orchestra of human longings, there exists a class frequently disregarded — the peaceful desires that stay underneath the surface, unpretentious murmurs of needs and needs that may not clatter for consideration but rather are by and by significant in their effect. These quiet desires, settled in the openings of the human mind, shape the complex scene of individual satisfaction and happiness. Investigating the domain of these calm desires requires a nuanced comprehension of the unobtrusive elements that impact human cravings and goals.

At the core of the calm desires lie the longings that may not adjust to cultural assumptions or outer approvals. Dissimilar to the more obvious goals that collect open acknowledgment, the peaceful desires work on an additional individual and cozy level. They are the cravings that people might wonder whether or not to explain transparently, either because of dread of judgment, cultural standards, or a feeling of weakness related with uncovering one's deepest desires.

These tranquil desires frequently manifest as well established interests, inventive tendencies, or eccentric dreams that may not line up with customary thoughts of accomplishment.

As far as some might be concerned, it could be the longing to seek after a creative undertaking, submerge themselves in a specialty interest, or leave on a modern profession way that reverberates with their bona fide selves. These cravings, however curbed, hold the way to opening a feeling of direction and individual fulfillment.

Besides, the peaceful desires stretch out past the domain of vocation and special goals to include the complexities of human connections. In the calm corners of the heart, people harbor a yearning for credible associations — connections described by certifiable figuring out, sympathy, and shared values. These social longings may not be verbalized unequivo-cally, yet they impact individuals decisions in framing and supporting associations with others.

The peaceful desires additionally track down articulation chasing isola-tion and thoughtfulness. In a world loaded up with commotion and steady network, the longing for snapshots of calm reflection and isolation turns into a significant longing. The need to withdraw from the requests of outside boosts, to track down comfort in one's own considerations, and to develop a profound association with oneself is a calm hanker-ing that frequently goes unnoticed yet holds tremendous importance for individual prosperity.

Disentangling the woven artwork of these peaceful desires includes stripping back layers of molding and cultural assumptions. The impacts of social standards, familial assumptions, and cultural benchmarks fre-quently shape people's longings in manners that may not line up with their bona fide selves. Perceiving and respecting these tranquil desires require a gutsy investigation of one's internal scene, an excursion that might include testing cultural standards and reclassifying individual meanings of progress and satisfaction.

In the expert domain, the calm desires might appear as a craving for significant work that goes past monetary achievement or cultural ac-knowledgment. People might long for a profession way that lines up with their qualities, takes into consideration imaginative articulation, or adds to a more prominent cultural great. These cravings, however unobtrusive, have the ability to reshape one's relationship with work, mixing it with reason and enthusiasm.

Besides, the calm desires frequently track down reverberation chasing self-improvement and self-disclosure. The longing to constantly develop, learn, and extend's comprehension one might interpret oneself is an inconspicuous yet strong power. This desire for self-development might lead people to look for new encounters, take part in reflective practices, or set out on an excursion of deep rooted learning, driven by an inward longing for individual satisfaction.

In the domain of close connections, the tranquil desires weave a sen-sitive string that interfaces people's personal scenes. The yearning for bona fide association, profound closeness, and a feeling of having a place frequently shape the calm inclinations of heartfelt cravings. These calm desires might incorporate the requirement for weakness, common help, and a common excursion of development with a soul mate.

Being a parent, as well, harbors its own arrangement of calm desires. Past the noticeable obligations and obvious articulations of adoration, guardians might long for snapshots of calm association with their kids, a profound comprehension of their special characters, and the capacity to support a climate where their youngsters can really put themselves out there. These unobtrusive cravings impact nurturing styles and shape the close to home bonds inside families.

With regards to cultural assumptions and social stories, the peaceful desires might collide with additional apparent and substantial markers of progress. The cultural accentuation on outer approval, material accomplishments, and predefined achievements frequently eclipses the meaning of these unobtrusive cravings. People might wind up conflicted between the quest for cultural endorsement and the calmer, more true desires that radiate from the inside.

The convergence of orientation assumptions and the calm desires adds one more layer of intricacy to the investigation of wants. Customary orientation jobs might force explicit assumptions on people, molding their desires and affecting the declaration of their legitimate selves. The tranquil desires that veer off from these gendered assumptions might confront obstruction or stay unacknowledged, featuring the requirement for a more comprehensive and sweeping comprehension of human cravings.

Exploring the landscape of the peaceful desires requires a sensitive dance among contemplation and outside investigation. It includes making a space for these inconspicuous cravings to arise, spread out, and be perceived without judgment. Developing mindfulness turns into a urgent part of respecting these calm desires — recognizing them as genuine and substantial parts of the human experience.

Besides, cultivating a culture that values credibility and urges people to communicate their calm desires adds to a more comprehensive and satisfying cultural scene. Perceiving and praising the different cluster of wants that exist past ordinary assumptions make ready for an aggregate shift towards a more broad comprehension of progress and satisfaction.

The tranquil desires, when let alone, may prompt a feeling of unfulfillment or an industrious yearning for something that stays slippery. On the other hand, recognizing and embracing these inconspicuous longings can be groundbreaking, opening ways to a daily existence that resounds all the more profoundly with one's credible self. It requires a cognizant decision to strip back the layers of cultural molding, outer assumptions, and the apprehension about judgment to uncover the tranquil desires that hold the way in to a really satisfying and significant presence.

The calm desires, however unpretentious, comprise an indispensable part of the human experience. They address the bona fide wants that may not adjust to cultural assumptions but rather are significant in their effect on private satisfaction and prosperity. Unwinding the complexities of these peaceful desires includes an excursion of self-disclosure, testing cultural standards, and making a space for true articulation.

By regarding these unpretentious desires, people leave on a way that prompts a more veritable and resounding life, where the ensemble of wants includes both the striking crescendos and the nuanced murmurs of the human spirit.

4.1 Unveiling the often-overlooked desires that children may not articulate.

Disclosing the Frequently Neglected Wants of Kids: Sustaining a More profound Comprehension of Their Inward Universes

Youth is a domain of unlimited creative mind, blamelessness, and an embroidery of wants that frequently wait underneath the surface, ready to be revealed. While kids may not generally articulate their needs and needs with accuracy, their inward universes are rich with goals, longings, and unobtrusive desires that add to the intricacy of their close to home scene. Investigating and understanding these frequently ignored wants requires a nuanced approach — one that rises above the superficial perceptions and digs into the mind boggling subtleties of kids' encounters.

At the core of the frequently disregarded wants of youngsters lies the requirement for certified association and profound articulation. From the earliest progressive phases, kids have an intrinsic craving for adoration, security, and a feeling of having a place. While these basic requirements are all around perceived, the particular subtleties of how kids look for and express these longings can shift broadly.

In the domain of profound articulation, youngsters might have wants that go past the apparent range of delight, bitterness, or outrage. The nuances of their profound world might incorporate a yearning for approval, understanding, or the opportunity to communicate many sentiments unafraid of judgment. Developing ability to understand people on a profound level in youngsters includes establishing a climate that recognizes and regards the profundity and variety of their close to home encounters.

Moreover, the frequently ignored wants of youngsters reach out into the space of independence and self-articulation. As people with one of a kind characters, interests, and viewpoints, youngsters harbor cravings for a feeling of organization over their lives. This might appear in a longing to decide, seek after unambiguous exercises, or put themselves out there in manners that mirror their true selves. Cultivating a climate that empowers and supports these cravings adds to the advancement of certain, confident people.

In the instructive setting, youngsters might hold onto longings for a learning climate that lines up with their singular styles and interests.

The frequently implicit longing for an educational plan that sparkles interest, cultivates inventiveness, and obliges different advancing requirements highlights the significance of fitting instructive ways to deal with the one of a kind cravings of every youngster. Perceiving and tending to these cravings can fundamentally influence a youngster's commitment and excitement for learning.

Besides, the frequently neglected wants of youngsters incorporate a longing for unstructured play and investigation. In a world progressively organized and driven by plans, kids may quietly pine for the opportunity to participate in unconstrained, creative play. This want reaches out past the quick delight of play; it sustains imagination, critical thinking abilities, and the improvement of a youngster's inward locus of control.

The frequently unpretentious cravings of kids likewise incorporate their requirement for valid associations with peers. While fellowships might appear to be straightforward on a superficial level, the longing for certifiable friendship, understanding, and a feeling of having a place can fundamentally impact a youngster's social encounters. Sustaining the social-close to home advancement of youngsters includes recognizing and tending to these frequently neglected wants inside the domain of companion connections.

Relational peculiarities assume a crucial part in uncovering the longings of youngsters. The craving for quality time, significant communications, and a conviction that all is good inside the nuclear family may not necessarily be unequivocally expressed by kids, however these longings significantly shape their impression of familial securities. Establishing a supporting family climate includes adjusting to these frequently implicit cravings and encouraging associations that focus on close to home prosperity.

Social and cultural impacts add layers to the frequently neglected wants of youngsters. The assumptions forced by cultural standards, social customs, and orientation jobs can shape youngsters' cravings in manners that may not line up with their genuine selves. Revealing these cravings requires a sharp consciousness of the outside impacts that might influence a kid's goals, considering a more nuanced comprehension of their longings inside the more extensive setting of their social and cultural environmental factors.

In the domain of innovation and advanced cooperations, the frequently ignored wants of kids might rotate around the requirement for balance. While advanced gadgets and online stages offer open doors for learning and amusement, youngsters may unobtrusively long for limits, disconnected encounters, and certified human associations. Recognizing these cravings includes exploring the computerized scene such that regards the all encompassing prosperity of youngsters.

Additionally, the frequently disregarded wants of youngsters stretch out into the area of self-disclosure and personality arrangement. As they explore the excursion of growing up, kids quietly wrestle with inquiries of self-personality, acknowledgment, and a craving to be perceived the truth about. Cultivating a climate that supports self-investigation, embraces variety, and celebrates independence adds to the solid improvement of a kid's identity.

Disclosing the frequently disregarded wants of kids requires a change in context — one that rises above the grown-up driven focal point through which their encounters are frequently deciphered. It requires undivided attention, sharp perception, and a veritable interest to comprehend the unpretentious signals and articulations that reveal the longings waiting inside the hearts of youngsters.

Guardians, parental figures, teachers, and society at large play significant jobs in perceiving and sustaining the frequently disregarded wants of youngsters. Making spaces that empower open correspondence, undivided attention, and a real interest in understanding the extraordinary characteristics of every kid prepares for divulging these cravings. The interaction includes a guarantee to establishing conditions that focus on the profound, social, and formative requirements of youngsters past the shallow or promptly evident parts of their lives.

Proceeding with the investigation of the frequently neglected wants of youngsters includes diving into the nuanced parts of their profound, mental, and social turn of events. Uncovering these cravings requires a significant comprehension of the unique exchange between individual contrasts, ecological impacts, and the developing idea of life as a youngster encounters.

Profound Flexibility and Methods for dealing with especially difficult times:

Kids quietly long for the apparatuses and methodologies to explore the intricacies of their feelings. The frequently neglected longing for close to home versatility appears in the requirement for direction on understanding and dealing with feelings successfully. Teachers, guardians, and guardians assume urgent parts in giving kids the profound jargon and survival strategies important to explore the promising and less promising times of life. Perceiving and addressing this want adds to the improvement of the ability to understand people on a profound level and furnishes youngsters with significant abilities for deep rooted prosperity.

Interest and the Affection for Learning:

At the center of experience growing up lies an intrinsic interest —
a hunger for information, investigation, and the delight of learning. The
frequently disregarded longing for scholarly excitement and a sustaining
climate that encourages interest is central to a youngster's mental turn of
events. Making instructive spaces that commend request, inventiveness,
and an adoration for learning respects this quiet hankering and establishes the groundwork for a deep rooted enthusiasm for information.

Nature and Open air Investigation:

Youngsters harbor a tranquil yearning for an association with nature
and the opportunity of outside investigation. In the advanced time of
screens and indoor exercises, the longing for unstructured play in regular
settings might be eclipsed. Recognizing and working with this frequently
disregarded want includes giving open doors to outside encounters, asso-
ciating with the normal world, and permitting kids to submerge themselves in the miracles of the climate.

Independence in Navigation:

The frequently implicit craving for independence arises as kids develop and foster an identity. While direction and backing are fundamental, youngsters quietly long for valuable chances to decide, express
inclinations, and experience a feeling of command over parts of their
lives. Perceiving and regarding this craving for independence adds to the
improvement of self-assurance, thinking abilities, and a solid feeling of
individual organization.

Social and Ethnic Character:

Youngsters explore the quiet excursion of understanding and embracing their social and ethnic personality. The frequently ignored longing for
social association and a feeling of having a place inside their social setting shapes their developing self-insight. Giving kids potential chances to
investigate and praise their social legacy, encouraging a comprehensive
climate, and recognizing different viewpoints add to a positive and certifying investigation of social personality.

Compassion and Social Mindfulness:

Youngsters have an intrinsic limit with regards to compassion and
social mindfulness, yet these characteristics might be eclipsed by other
formative achievements. The frequently ignored craving for direction in
exploring social elements, figuring out others' viewpoints, and creating
significant associations is vital to their social-profound development.
Supporting these characteristics includes advancing benevolence, showing compromise, and encouraging a merciful comprehension of different
encounters.

Articulation of Inventiveness:

Inventiveness streams easily inside the domain of young life, where creative mind exceeds all rational limitations. The frequently implicit craving for roads to communicate inventiveness — whether through workmanship, narrating, or innovative play — dwells inside each kid. Cultivating conditions that empower imaginative articulation, celebrate different types of imaginative investigation, and worth the extraordinary commitments of every youngster praises this quiet hankering for innovative satisfaction.

Solid Relationship with Innovation:

In the computerized age, youngsters harbor a frequently ignored longing for a solid relationship with innovation.

The quiet longing for direction in exploring computerized spaces, understanding the effect of innovation on their prosperity, and cultivating a harmony between screen time and genuine encounters highlights the requirement for a careful way to deal with innovation use in youth.

Solid Self-perception and Self-Acknowledgment:

As youngsters foster a healthy identity, they quietly explore the frequently muddled landscape of self-perception and self-acknowledgment. The longing for positive self-perception and confidence is woven into the texture of their advancing personalities. Establishing conditions that advance body inspiration, variety, and self-acknowledgment adds to the improvement of a sound mental self portrait and strong confidence.

Cheerful Association with Development and Play:

Youngsters have a natural longing for upbeat development and play. The frequently neglected longing for unrestrained chuckling, actual work, and uninhibited play might be veiled by organized timetables and scholarly requests. Perceiving and focusing on the significance of play and development in youth adds to comprehensive turn of events, encouraging actual wellbeing, and supporting the sheer euphoria that comes from dynamic commitment.

In the excursion of revealing the frequently disregarded wants of youngsters, appreciating the interconnected idea of these quiet yearnings is vital. Youngsters' encounters are complex, and their longings range across close to home, mental, social, and actual aspects. A comprehensive methodology includes perceiving the exceptional characteristics of every youngster, encouraging conditions that honor different goals, and developing a profound comprehension of the complex embroidery that shapes their singular processes.

Guardians, parental figures, teachers, and society at large are instrumental in making spaces that permit these frequently quiet longings to surface and be tended to. Undivided attention, open correspondence, and a promise to understanding the developing necessities of youngsters structure the establishment for a steady and supporting climate. By recognizing and answering the frequently disregarded wants of youngsters, we add to the development of strong, mindful, and genuinely expressive people who are engaged to explore the intricacies of experience growing up and then some. In embracing the quiet desires of kids, we set out on an aggregate excursion of supporting the cutting edge with compassion, shrewdness, and a significant appreciation for the extravagance of their internal universes.

4.2 Discussing the difference between expressed wants and unspoken needs.

Investigating the Mind boggling Interaction Between Communicated Needs and Implicit Necessities: Exploring the Profundities of Human Cravings

Human longings are unpredictable, multi-layered, and frequently imparted through a double focal point — communicated needs and implicit necessities. This nuanced exchange between what people expressly state they need and the fundamental, some of the time stowed away, needs they may not well-spoken presents a rich scene for grasping the intricacy of human desires. Digging into this mind boggling domain includes unwinding the layers that separate communicated needs from implicit requirements, perceiving the powerful connection between the two, and understanding how this exchange shapes individual encounters and relational elements.

Communicated Needs: The Surface Sign of Wants

Communicated needs are the plain, expressed articulations of wants — what people intentionally convey as their inclinations, wishes, or desires. These can go from unmistakable material needs, like a craving for another device or a particular thing, to additional theoretical longings, like the wish for acknowledgment, achievement, or significant connections. Communicated needs are many times molded by outer impacts, cultural assumptions, and quick conditions.

With regards to relational connections, communicated needs turned into a pivotal part of correspondence. People articulate their requirements and wants to pass on inclinations, lay out limits, or look for satisfaction. This immediate type of correspondence fills in as an aide for exploring shared spaces, whether in familial, heartfelt, or proficient connections. For instance, an individual might communicate a need for greater quality time with an accomplice, flagging the significance of association and shared encounters.

Communicated needs are likewise clear in cultural designs, where people convey their yearnings for progress, approval, or achievement. These verbalized longings add to the forming of individual objectives, profession ways, and the quest for cultural benchmarks. The acknowledgment of communicated needs on both individual and cultural levels shapes the reason for useful discourse, objective setting, and the foundation of shared values.

Nonetheless, the superficial idea of communicated needs frequently gives just a halfway perspective on the multifaceted embroidery of human longings. It is in the investigation of implicit necessities that a more profound, more nuanced comprehension of individual desires arises.

Implicit Requirements: The Underground Flows of Want

Implicit requirements dwell underneath the surface, appearing as inconspicuous propensities that impact contemplations, feelings, and ways of behaving. Not at all like communicated needs, implicit requirements are not generally promptly clear or imparted in a direct way. They might be established in profound, mental, or existential aspects, reflecting center parts of a singular's character and prosperity.

These implicit necessities frequently originate from principal human cravings for association, having a place, security, and self-realization. The intricacy of implicit requirements is increased by their abstract and profoundly private nature. For instance, an individual might hold onto an implicit requirement for approval, looking for confirmation and acknowledgment as a crucial part of their self-esteem.

In relational connections, implicit requirements can shape the elements between people. An individual might have an implicit requirement for consistent reassurance during testing times, a craving for understanding, or a yearning for closeness that goes past the outer layer of communicated needs. Perceiving and tending to these implicit necessities requires an elevated degree of compassion, attunement, and an eagerness to participate in more profound, more thoughtful discussions.

Implicit requirements additionally stretch out into the domain of self-awareness and self-revelation. People might convey implicit requirements for self-realization, significance, and satisfaction that drive their decisions, interests, and life directions. The affirmation of these more profound, inborn longings frames the establishment for a more all encompassing and true way to deal with self-awareness.

The Interchange: Exploring the Intricate Relationship

The transaction between communicated needs and implicit necessities is a dynamic and at times fragile dance that shapes human encounters. It is fundamental to perceive that these two features of want are not totally unrelated; all things being equal, they coincide, affecting each other in mind boggling ways. Understanding the interchange requires a nuanced viewpoint that thinks about the inspirations, setting, and basic feelings that add to the outflow of needs and the sign of implicit necessities.

In certain examples, communicated needs act as immediate appearances of implicit necessities. For instance, an individual communicating a craving for monetary achievement might be driven by an implicit requirement for security and steadiness. Perceiving the connection between the superficial need and the hidden need gives knowledge into the persuasive powers at play and considers a more thorough comprehension of individual goals.

On the other hand, there are circumstances where communicated needs might separate from implicit requirements. This misalignment can happen because of outer impacts, cultural assumptions, or an absence of mindfulness. For example, an individual communicating a longing for material belongings might be concealing an implicit requirement for close to home satisfaction or association. Exploring these cases requires a delicate investigation of the inspirations driving communicated needs, reassuring people to dig into the more profound layers of their longings.

With regards to relational connections, the transaction between communicated needs and implicit requirements turns out to be especially critical. Miscommunication or an inability to perceive the basic necessities can prompt false impressions, neglected assumptions, and social strain. On the other hand, when people in a relationship are sensitive to both the communicated needs and implicit requirements of their accomplices, it cultivates a more profound association, common comprehension, and the capacity to explore difficulties with compassion and backing.

The cultural setting assumes a significant part in forming the transaction between communicated needs and implicit requirements. Social standards, cultural assumptions, and outside tensions can impact the manner in which people articulate their cravings and the degree to which they feel open to communicating their more profound requirements. Developing a cultural climate that values legitimacy, empowers open exchange, and regards the variety of human longings adds to a more strong and figuring out aggregate culture.

Exploring the Intricacy: Techniques for Understanding and Regarding Wants

Exploring the complex connection between communicated needs and implicit necessities requires a blend of mindfulness, sympathetic correspondence, and a guarantee to cultivating valid associations. People, as well as those in connections and cultural designs, can utilize techniques to really explore this intricacy more:

Develop Mindfulness:

Empowering self-reflection and contemplation empowers people to acquire understanding into their communicated needs and implicit necessities. This mindfulness frames the establishment for more true self-articulation and a more profound comprehension of individual cravings.

Advance Open Correspondence:

Cultivating a climate of open correspondence is fundamental for exploring the transaction between communicated needs and implicit requirements in connections. Empowering people to verbalize their longings, while additionally making space for more profound discussions about hidden needs, improves social elements.

Practice Undivided attention:

Effectively paying attention to both the communicated needs and implicit signals in correspondence is urgent for grasping the intricacy of wants. Focusing on non-verbal signs, feelings, and unobtrusive articulations gives important experiences into hidden needs.

Energize Sympathy:

Developing sympathy includes recognizing and approving the feelings and wants communicated by others. Understanding the point of view of people with regards to their more profound requirements adds to additional caring and steady connections.

Make a Culture of Credibility:

Cultural designs can add to a culture that values credibility by empowering people to communicate their cravings unafraid of judgment. Perceiving and regarding assorted articulations of needs and needs encourages a comprehensive and grasping cultural climate.

Embrace Adaptability:

Perceiving that wants are dynamic and may advance over the long run considers more noteworthy adaptability in exploring the exchange between communicated needs and implicit necessities. Embracing flexibility and a readiness to reevaluate wants adds to self-improvement and social strength.

Advance Ability to appreciate people at their core:

Creating the ability to appreciate people on a deeper level includes understanding one's own feelings as well as being receptive to the feelings of others. This increased mindfulness adds to a more nuanced comprehension of the longings communicated and implicit requirements inside relational connections.

Look for Proficient Help:

In circumstances where the intricacy of wants presents difficulties, looking for proficient help from advisors, advocates, or relationship specialists can give significant direction. Proficient intercessions offer an organized space for investigating wants, cultivating correspondence, and exploring social elements.

By consolidating these systems, people and those in connections can explore the multifaceted exchange between communicated needs and implicit necessities with more noteworthy mindfulness and awareness. The acknowledgment of the intricacy innate in human longings adds to the formation of better, additional satisfying connections and a cultural culture that esteems the legitimacy of individual goals.

Proceeding with our investigation of the unpredictable interaction between communicated needs and implicit requirements, it is fundamental to dive further into explicit situations and settings where this unique relationship unfurls.

This extra investigation will reveal insight into the assorted manners by which human longings manifest and the nuanced manners by which people explore the intricacies of their needs and needs.

In Connections:
The elements of communicated needs and implicit necessities assume a crucial part in forming the scene of relational connections. Couples, families, and companions explore a sensitive harmony between expressed wants and the hidden, once in a while verifiable, needs that impact their communications.

In heartfelt connections, for example, an accomplice might communicate a longing for greater quality time together. While this is an unmistakable enunciated need, the implicit need might include a more profound desire for close to home association, closeness, or consolation. By perceiving and tending to the two perspectives — the communicated need and the implicit need — couples can encourage a more profound comprehension of one another's close to home scenes.

Relational peculiarities, as well, are fundamentally impacted by the interchange between communicated needs and implicit necessities. Guardians might communicate a need for their youngsters to succeed scholastically, determined by an implicit requirement for their kids' prosperity and prosperity. Understanding this dynamic takes into account more sympathetic nurturing, taking into account the communicated need as well as the basic inspirations and requirements that impact family yearnings.

In fellowships, people might communicate needs for shared encounters or explicit sorts of help, while implicit necessities might include a longing for certifiable association, unwaveringness, or a feeling of having a place. Perceiving and respecting both the express cravings and the inconspicuous inclinations of companionship adds to the profundity and legitimacy of these connections.

In the Working environment:
The expert domain is one more field where the interaction between communicated needs and implicit requirements essentially impacts

individual fulfillment, group elements, and hierarchical culture. Representatives might verbalize needs, for example, professional success, pay increments, or adaptable work courses of action, mirroring their goals inside the working environment.

Nonetheless, underneath these communicated needs lie implicit necessities attached to a longing for acknowledgment, a feeling of direction in their work, or a requirement for a strong and comprehensive workplace. Associations that focus on getting it and tending to both the communicated needs and implicit necessities of their representatives encourage a culture of worker commitment, fulfillment, and efficiency.

Authority elements inside associations are especially impacted by this interaction. A pioneer might communicate a need for expanded group execution, yet the implicit need might include a longing for the group's acknowledgment of their initiative style or a requirement for a cooperative and strong work culture. Perceiving these subtleties takes into consideration initiative that isn't just outcomes driven yet in addition sensitive to the more profound requirements of both the pioneer and the group.

In Self-improvement:

The excursion of self-improvement and self-disclosure is complicatedly associated with the interchange between communicated needs and implicit requirements. People frequently leave on ways of personal development by defining unequivocal objectives and desires — communicated needs that might incorporate obtaining new abilities, seeking after instructive undertakings, or accomplishing explicit achievements.

However, underneath these objectives lie implicit requirements for individual satisfaction, a feeling of direction, and the continuous journey for self-realization. Understanding the inspirations driving these communicated maintains that permits people should adjust their self-awareness excursions to their more profound, more inherent longings, prompting a more credible and satisfying life.

Besides, implicit requirements might appear as a longing for flexibility, profound prosperity, or a feeling of having a place inside one's own personality. These unsaid necessities guide people toward practices like care, taking care of oneself, and significant associations that add to their all encompassing prosperity.

In Social and Cultural Settings:

The exchange between communicated needs and implicit necessities stretches out to more extensive social and cultural settings, molding aggregate yearnings, standards, and assumptions. Cultural designs frequently underscore specific communicated needs, like material achievement, magnificence norms, or explicit accomplishments, affecting individual goals and wants.

Be that as it may, underneath these cultural assumptions lie implicit requirements for inclusivity, acknowledgment, and a feeling of having a place. People might communicate needs that adjust to cultural standards yet harbor implicit requirements for validness, variety, and the opportunity to seek after their remarkable ways.

Social characters are complicatedly woven into this transaction, as people express needs attached to social pride, customs, or explicit markers of accomplishment. Implicit requirements inside social settings might include a longing for grasping, affirmation, and the protection of social legacy. Perceiving and regarding these nuanced elements encourages a more comprehensive and socially touchy society.

Procedures for Exploring the Interaction:

Exploring the mind boggling interaction between communicated needs and implicit necessities requires a bunch of techniques that advance grasping, compassion, and genuineness:

Undivided attention:

Effectively paying attention to both the communicated needs and implicit signals in correspondence is basic for grasping the intricacy of wants. This includes focusing not exclusively to verbal articulations yet in addition to non-verbal signs, feelings, and unobtrusive subtleties.

Open Correspondence:

Cultivating a climate of open correspondence urges people to truly communicate their longings more. This incorporates making spaces for discourse where both express needs and certain necessities can be enunciated without judgment.

Compassion and Viewpoint Taking:

Developing compassion includes recognizing and approving the feelings and wants communicated by others. Viewpoint taking permits people to grasp the inspirations driving both the communicated needs and implicit requirements, adding to additional merciful connections.

Develop Mindfulness:

People benefit from developing mindfulness to grasp their own cravings, inspirations, and the likely misalignment between communicated needs and implicit requirements. This contemplative interaction empowers more credible self-articulation.

Careful Reflection:

Taking part in careful reflection includes considering the more deeply inspirations and necessities that underlie communicated needs. This intelligent practice adds to a more nuanced comprehension of wants and an increased familiarity with their intricacy.

Advance a Culture of Genuineness:

Cultural designs and associations can add to a culture that values genuineness by recognizing and regarding different articulations of needs and needs. This includes making comprehensive spaces that permit people to be consistent with themselves.

Energize All encompassing Objective Setting:

In private and expert settings, objective setting ought to envelop both communicated needs and implicit requirements. This comprehensive methodology permits people to seek after yearnings that line up with their more profound cravings, encouraging a feeling of direction and satisfaction.

Look for Common Grasping in Connections:

In connections, whether heartfelt, familial, or proficient, looking for common comprehension includes perceiving and regarding the cravings of others. This incorporates making an exchange that takes into consideration the investigation of both communicated needs and implicit necessities.

Embracing the Intricacy of Human Cravings

Our investigation of the exchange between communicated needs and implicit necessities, it is obvious that the lavishness of human longings lies in their intricacy. Understanding the multifaceted dance between what people expressly state they need and the more profound, frequently covered up, needs they may not well-spoken is fundamental for cultivating genuineness, compassion, and significant associations.

Communicated needs act as the noticeable signs of wants, reflecting prompt inclinations, objectives, and goals. Implicit necessities, then again, dwell underneath the surface, directing people toward inborn desires attached to character, association, and prosperity.

Exploring this transaction requires a nuanced approach — one that includes undivided attention, open correspondence, compassion, and a pledge to encouraging validness. It includes perceiving that wants are dynamic, developing, and profoundly private, formed by a horde of impacts, including social, cultural, and individual elements.

In connections, the working environment, self-awareness, and social settings, people and networks benefit from embracing the intricacy of wants. This includes recognizing the conjunction of communicated needs and implicit requirements, understanding the inspirations driving both, and making spaces that honor the legitimacy of individual yearnings.

As we explore the embroidery of human cravings, we set out on an excursion of self-disclosure, common comprehension, and the development of connections that reverberate with genuineness. It is in this hug of intricacy that we open the potential for more extravagant, additional satisfying lives, both for us and inside the perplexing trap of human associations. In regarding the transaction between communicated needs and implicit requirements, we commend the significant profundity and variety of the human experience.

4.3 Showcasing instances where identifying these desires transformed parent-child dynamics.

Extraordinary Elements: The Force of Distinguishing and Sustaining Youngsters' Longings inside Parent-Kid Connections

The parent-kid relationship is a significant and developing excursion set apart by adoration, direction, and common development.

Inside this perplexing dance, understanding and recognizing the longings of youngsters — both communicated and implicit — hold the way to groundbreaking elements. Cases flourish where guardians, outfitted with understanding into their kids' desires and basic requirements, have guided the course of nurturing towards more profound associations, improved correspondence, and the sustaining of a kid's credible self. This investigation digs into piercing models that grandstand the force of perceiving and answering youngsters' longings inside the setting of parent-kid connections.

1. Cultivating Scholastic Excitement:

    In the domain of schooling, recognizing a youngster's longings can fundamentally influence their scholarly excursion. Consider the instance of a little kid named Emily who, in spite of having a distinct fascination with workmanship and imagination, ended up striving inside an ordinary instructive setting that focused on state sanctioned testing and unbending educational program structures. Emily's folks, receptive to her implicit requirement for a really supporting climate, chose to investigate elective instructive methodologies that embraced her imaginative tendencies.

    Enlisting Emily in a school that coordinated expressions into the educational plan changed her scholastic experience as well as touched off a newly discovered excitement for learning. The acknowledgment of Emily's implicit requirement for a more customized instructive methodology tended to her longing for innovative articulation as well as reinforced her confidence and in general scholarly execution. This occurrence delineates how distinguishing and answering a kid's implicit longings can prompt a more agreeable and satisfying instructive excursion.

2. Supporting Autonomy:

    As youngsters develop, the craving for independence and freedom turns into a huge part of their turn of events. Sarah, a teen exploring the sensitive harmony among reliance and freedom, communicated her need to settle on conclusions about her own life and decisions. Sarah's folks, perceiving the hidden implicit requirement for independence, took part in open conversations about direction and obligation.

By encouraging a climate that permitted Sarah to steadily take on additional obligations and pursue informed decisions, her folks regarded her communicated need for freedom as well as sustained her implicit requirement for a feeling of command over her life. This groundbreaking methodology fortified the parent-kid bond as well as furnished Sarah with important thinking abilities and a developing identity viability.

3. **Developing Profound Versatility:**
   Youngsters frequently wrestle with a bunch of feelings that might slip through the cracks underneath the surface. Jenny, a ten-year-old, showed periodic eruptions of disappointment and withdrawal.

   While her communicated need was many times a longing for more recess, her implicit need uncovered a more profound battle with handling feelings and building close to home flexibility. Jenny's folks, distinctly attentive of her close to home signals, presented exercises that encouraged profound articulation and correspondence.

   Through workmanship treatment and open discussions about sentiments, Jenny's implicit requirement for everyday encouragement was met. The extraordinary effect was obvious as Jenny displayed better close to home guideline as well as fostered a more hearty profound jargon. This occurrence highlights the significance of perceiving and tending to a youngster's implicit cravings for profound prosperity, adding to the development of long lasting capacity to understand people on a deeper level.

4. **Observing Different Abilities:**
   Youngsters innately have one of a kind gifts and interests that may not necessarily line up with conventional assumptions. Alex, a twelve-year-old enthusiastically for coding and innovation, ended up attempting to accommodate his affection for these pursuits with cultural assumptions that stressed scholarly accomplishment in additional conventional subjects. Alex's folks, sensitive to his implicit requirement for acknowledgment and approval of his extraordinary gifts, effectively supported and praised his advantage in innovation.

   By selecting Alex in coding classes, taking part in innovation related projects together, and displaying his accomplishments to loved ones, his folks respected his communicated need for acknowledgment as well as supported his implicit requirement for acknowledgment and approval. The extraordinary effect was obvious in Alex's developing certainty, a deep satisfaction in his capacities, and a reinforced parent-youngster bond based on common regard for individual gifts.

5. Exploring Social Elements:
Kids frequently wrestle with the intricacies of social collaborations and fellowships, exploring implicit longings for association, acknowledgment, and a feeling of having a place. Mia, a thirteen-year-old, communicated a believe for additional open doors should associate with her companions. Nonetheless, her folks, mindful of the implicit requirement for direction in exploring social elements, started open discussions about companionships, peer pressure, and powerful correspondence.

By tending to Mia's implicit requirement for social direction, her folks gave important bits of knowledge as well as reinforced the parent-youngster relationship through open exchange. The groundbreaking effect reached out past Mia's social communications, affecting her capacity to explore associations with sympathy and flexibility.

6. Supporting Inventiveness and Creative mind:
Youngsters are innately inventive creatures, and their implicit cravings frequently rotate around the requirement for imaginative articulation and unstructured play. Jake, a seven-year-old with a distinctive creative mind, frequently communicated his need for additional opportunity to play with his toys and participate in creative exercises. Perceiving Jake's implicit requirement for imaginative outlets, his folks changed their way to deal with recess.

By integrating narrating, innovative play, and imaginative exercises into Jake's daily schedule, his folks respected his communicated need for play as well as sustained his implicit requirement for inventive articulation. The extraordinary effect was obvious as Jake created improved inventiveness, critical thinking abilities, and a more profound appreciation for the force of creative mind.

7. Exploring Advanced Spaces Carefully:
In the advanced age, youngsters' longings frequently stretch out into the domain of innovation and online connections. Emma, a fourteen-year-old, communicated a need for more screen time and admittance to online entertainment stages. Perceiving her implicit requirement for direction in exploring advanced spaces capably, Emma's folks took part in open discussions about web-based security, computerized citizenship, and the effect of innovation on prosperity.

By tending to Emma's implicit requirement for computerized proficiency and dependable internet based conduct, her folks encouraged a more secure web-based climate as well as imparted values that rose above Emma's nearby need for expanded screen time. The groundbreaking effect was apparent in Emma's careful way to deal with advanced cooperations, understanding the possible outcomes and obligations related with online presence.

8. Respecting Social Personality:

Kids frequently wrestle with a craving for association with their social character, a viewpoint that might go implicit yet fundamentally impacts their healthy identity. Olivia, a twelve-year-old from a multicultural foundation, communicated a need for additional contribution in social festivals and customs. Her folks, receptive to her implicit requirement for a more profound association with her social personality, effectively participated in social exercises, shared stories, and celebrated customs as a family.

By regarding Olivia's communicated need for social contribution and tending to her implicit requirement for a feeling of having a place, her folks improved how she might interpret social legacy as well as reinforced the family security through shared encounters. The extraordinary effect stretched out past Olivia's singular process, adding to an aggregate appreciation for social variety inside the family.

Proceeding with our investigation of extraordinary parent-youngster elements from the perspective of distinguishing and answering kids' cravings, how about we dive into extra situations that highlight the significant effect of this methodology. These occurrences further enlighten the nuanced exchange between communicated needs and implicit necessities, exhibiting how guardians, furnished with knowledge and compassion, can shape positive and enduring changes inside the parent-kid relationship.

9. Exploring Execution Strain:

Kids frequently wrestle with the strain to succeed scholastically or in extracurricular exercises. Michael, a fifteen-year-old, reliably communicated a need for high grades and accomplishments. Nonetheless, his folks, sensitive to his implicit requirement for a decent and strong methodology, started discussions about the significance of exertion, strength, and prosperity over persistent quest for flawlessness.

By tending to Michael's implicit requirement for a reasonable viewpoint on progress, his folks lightened execution tension as well as imparted upsides of taking care of oneself and a solid hard working attitude. The groundbreaking effect was clear as Michael fostered a more feasible way to deal with his investigations and extracurricular pursuits, encouraging a feeling of satisfaction past outer accomplishments.

10. **Empowering Articulation of Feelings:**

    Youngsters' personal scenes are huge and shifted, frequently requiring a nuanced understanding from guardians. Sarah, a nine-year-old, much of the time displayed a longing for more recess as a method for adapting to personal difficulties. Perceiving her implicit requirement for close to home articulation, Sarah's folks acquainted exercises that permitted her with articulate her sentiments through workmanship, narrating, and play.

    By tending to Sarah's implicit requirement for profound outlets, her folks gave a productive means to articulation as well as cultivated capacity to understand people at their core and versatility. The extraordinary effect reached out past Sarah's close to home prosperity, adding to a family culture that esteemed open correspondence and sympathy.

11. **Cultivating an Adoration for Nature:**

    Youngsters' association with the normal world frequently remains closely connected with implicit cravings for investigation, interest, and a feeling of marvel. Ethan, a twelve-year-old, communicated a need for additional open air exercises. Perceiving his implicit requirement for a more profound association with nature, Ethan's folks coordinated family climbs, setting up camp excursions, and nature-based trips.

    By addressing Ethan's implicit requirement for an association with the outside, his folks sustained an affection for nature as well as set out open doors for family holding and shared encounters. The extraordinary effect was obvious as Ethan fostered a feeling of ecological stewardship and an elevated appreciation for the excellence of the regular world.

12. **Supporting Kin Connections:**

    Kin frequently explore complex elements that include a craving for friendship, shared encounters, and compromise. Lily, a thirteen-year-old, communicated a need for additional positive cooperations with her more youthful sibling. Perceiving her implicit requirement for direction in exploring kin connections, Lily's folks worked with family conversations on viable correspondence, compassion, and compromise.

    By tending to Lily's implicit requirement for help in kin elements, her folks reinforced the kin bond as well as outfitted Lily with relational abilities that stretched out past the family setting. The extraordinary effect added to a more agreeable family climate based on shared regard and understanding.

13. **Cultivating Comprehensive Qualities:**
Youngsters frequently incorporate cultural qualities and standards, which might impact their communicated needs and implicit necessities. Alex, a sixteen-year-old, communicated a craving for additional inclusivity and acknowledgment inside peer gatherings. Perceiving his implicit requirement for direction on developing comprehensive qualities, Alex's folks started discussions about variety, compassion, and the significance of embracing contrasts.

By tending to Alex's implicit requirement for a more profound comprehension of inclusivity, his folks added to a positive friend climate as well as imparted upsides of compassion and acknowledgment. The groundbreaking effect stretched out past Alex's nearby group of friends, affecting his point of view on inclusivity inside more extensive cultural settings.

14. **Adjusting Extracurricular Requests:**
Kids frequently take part in different extracurricular exercises, each mirroring an extraordinary arrangement of wants and needs. Ava, a fourteen-year-old, communicated a need for contribution in different extracurricular pursuits. Perceiving her implicit requirement for equilibrium and taking care of oneself, Ava's folks participated in discussions no time like the present administration, needs, and the significance of balanced improvement.

By addressing Ava's implicit requirement for a fair way to deal with extracurricular exercises, her folks upheld her self-awareness as well as ingrained upsides of mindfulness and comprehensive prosperity. The groundbreaking effect was clear as Ava fostered a more deliberate way to deal with her interests, encouraging flexibility and a feeling of individual satisfaction.

15. **Exploring Orientation Generalizations:**

Youngsters might wrestle with cultural assumptions connected with orientation jobs and articulations. Riley, a twelve-year-old, communicated a need for more opportunity in picking clothing styles and interests generally connected with the contrary orientation. Perceiving Riley's implicit requirement for acknowledgment and understanding, Riley's folks participated in discussions about distinction, self-articulation, and breaking liberated from orientation generalizations.

By tending to Riley's implicit requirement for approval and backing in exploring orientation character, Riley's folks not just encouraged a feeling of acknowledgment inside the family yet additionally added to a more comprehensive point of view on orientation jobs. The extraordinary effect stretched out past Riley's own excursion, impacting a more extensive comprehension of variety and acknowledgment.

An Embroidery of Extraordinary Minutes

In these different situations, the acknowledgment and reaction to youngsters' longings — both communicated and implicit — arise as impetuses for extraordinary elements inside parent-kid connections. Each occasion features the significant effect of parental attunement, compassion, and proactive commitment to figuring out the many-sided embroidered artwork of kids' yearnings and necessities.

The continuous excursion of change inside parent-youngster elements requires a pledge to progressing perception, open correspondence, and flexibility. Guardians, as guides and mates, explore this excursion with a comprehension that every youngster's longings are special, developing, and profoundly attached to their healthy identity.

As we consider these extraordinary minutes, it becomes obvious that the parent-kid relationship is a powerful material where the strings of communicated needs and implicit necessities interlace. This interchange shapes the prompt encounters of experience growing up as well as lays the preparation for deep rooted examples of correspondence, understanding, and shared regard.

In praising the force of recognizing and answering kids' longings, guardians leave on an excursion set apart by development, association, and the common formation of a family story. These extraordinary minutes act as building blocks for strong, compassionate, and legitimately expressive people who, thus, add to the rich woven artwork of human association and understanding.

Chapter 5

Navigating Emotional Terrain

Exploring the Close to home Landscape: Understanding, Communicating, and Flourishing in the Domain of Feelings

Feelings structure the mind boggling scene of human experience, molding our discernments, choices, and communications. Exploring the profound territory is a complex excursion that includes grasping the scope of feelings, communicating them legitimately, and developing capacity to understand people on a deeper level for individual and relational development. In this investigation, we dig into the intricacy of feelings, the meaning of close to home articulation, and the extraordinary force of creating the ability to understand people on a profound level.

Figuring out the Range of Feelings:

The range of human feelings is immense and nuanced, including a wide exhibit of sentiments that reach from satisfaction and love to bitterness, outrage, and dread. Every inclination fills in as an open sign, giving experiences into our interior states and reactions to outer boosts. Understanding this close to home range includes recognizing the legitimacy and variety of sentiments, both positive and testing.

Positive feelings, like satisfaction and appreciation, add to prosperity and strength. They frequently mirror a feeling of achievement, association, or fulfillment. Then again, testing feelings, similar to misery and outrage, signal neglected needs, unfulfilled assumptions, or reactions to saw dangers. Perceiving the intricacy of feelings includes embracing their complex nature and reexamining them as significant couriers instead of simple responses.

The Significance of Profound Articulation:

Profound articulation is a central part of exploring the close to home territory. Real articulation permits people to impart their sentiments, cultivating mindfulness and setting out open doors for association with others. The concealment or disavowal of feelings can prompt unseen fits of turmoil, affecting mental and actual prosperity. Understanding the meaning of profound articulation includes developing a sound connection with one's sentiments and making spaces for open correspondence.

Communicating feelings legitimately includes both verbal and non-verbal correspondence. Verbal articulation incorporates articulating sentiments through words, whether in discussions, composed structure, or creative articulation. Non-verbal prompts, like looks, non-verbal communication, and signals, likewise assume a critical part in conveying feelings. The two types of articulation add to the lavishness of human correspondence and the mutual perspective of profound encounters.

Developing Capacity to appreciate people at their core:

The capacity to appreciate people on a profound level (EI) is the capacity to perceive, comprehend, and deal with one's own feelings while likewise relating to the feelings of others. Developing capacity to understand individuals on a profound level is a groundbreaking excursion that includes self-reflection, compassion improvement, and the refinement of relational abilities. People with high capacity to appreciate anyone on a deeper level explore the close to home landscape with more noteworthy flexibility, shaping better connections and pursuing informed choices.

Mindfulness:

The groundwork of the capacity to appreciate anyone on a profound level lies in mindfulness — the capacity to perceive and grasp one's own feelings. This includes reflection, care, and a continuous investigation of interior states. Developing mindfulness permits people to distinguish examples, triggers, and the basic inspirations driving their feelings.

Self-Guideline:

Self-guideline is the ability to oversee and balance close to home reactions. This part of the ability to appreciate anyone at their core includes methods, for example, profound breathing, care rehearses, and mental reappraisal to explore testing feelings. By creating self-guideline abilities, people can answer circumstances with more prominent lucidity and flexibility, keeping away from rash responses.

Inspiration:

Inspiration inside the domain of the capacity to appreciate people on a deeper level connects with the capacity to outfit feelings for productive purposes. This includes laying out and chasing after objectives, keeping an uplifting perspective, and utilizing inherent inspiration to explore difficulties. Genuinely insightful people influence their profound states as wellsprings of motivation and assurance.

Sympathy:

Sympathy is the ability to comprehend and talk about the thoughts of others. Developing sympathy includes undivided attention, viewpoint taking, and the capacity to interface with the feelings of people around us. Sympathetic people add to steady and merciful relational elements, cultivating further associations with others.

Interactive abilities:

Interactive abilities envelop compelling correspondence, compromise, and the capacity to explore social circumstances with class and awareness. Creating interactive abilities inside the setting of the capacity to appreciate anyone on a deeper level upgrades relational connections, establishing conditions that support cooperation, understanding, and shared profound encounters.

Exploring Testing Feelings:

Testing feelings, frequently named as "pessimistic," assume a pivotal part in the profound territory. Exploring these feelings includes recognizing their presence, figuring out their beginnings, and creating valuable ways of tending to them. Concealment or evasion of testing feelings can prompt long haul pessimistic consequences for emotional wellness.

Figuring out Outrage:

Outrage, a strong and frequently misjudged feeling, can flag limits being crossed, neglected needs, or saw treacheries. Exploring outrage includes perceiving its triggers, investigating fundamental causes, and directing its energy into useful activities. Solid articulations of outrage can prompt self-assuredness, limit setting, and positive change.

Embracing Misery:

Misery is a characteristic reaction to misfortune, disillusionment, or unfulfilled assumptions. As opposed to staying away from trouble, exploring this feeling includes permitting oneself to lament, looking for help, and taking part in exercises that advance recuperating. Embracing misery adds to profound versatility and a more profound comprehension of individual necessities.

Overseeing Dread and Tension:

Dread and tension frequently emerge in light of seen dangers or vulnerabilities. Exploring these feelings includes creating methods for dealing with especially difficult times, like care, unwinding procedures, and re-evaluating pessimistic idea designs. Overseeing dread and nervousness adds to a feeling of strengthening and the capacity to confront difficulties with more prominent flexibility.

Tending to Coerce and Disgrace:

Culpability and disgrace can come from a feeling of moral offense or saw insufficiency. Exploring these feelings includes recognizing liability where proper, looking for pardoning, and participating in self-sympathy.

Addressing responsibility and disgrace permits people to gain from botches while cultivating self-acknowledgment.

Groundbreaking Force of Close to home Articulation in Connections:

The nature of relational connections is profoundly affected by the capacity to communicate and explore feelings actually. Correspondence inside connections includes the trading of data as well as the sharing of close to home encounters. The extraordinary force of close to home articulation in connections is clear in different aspects:

Building Association:

Genuine profound articulation cultivates a feeling of association between people. Sharing sentiments, weaknesses, and delights makes a close to home bond that rises above shallow collaborations. In heartfelt connections, fellowships, and familial associations, the capacity to communicate and get feelings reinforces the texture of the relationship.

Compromise:

Profound articulation assumes an essential part in settling clashes inside connections. Open correspondence about sentiments, points of view, and needs permits people to valuably explore conflicts. The extraordinary effect of close to home articulation in compromise lies in encouraging grasping, split the difference, and common development.

Cultivating Compassion:

Genuinely expressive people add to the improvement of compassion inside connections. The capacity to lucid and share one's close to home encounters upgrades the comprehension of others' points of view. Sympathy, thus, establishes a strong and merciful climate where people feel appreciated and esteemed.

Advancing Profound Wellbeing:

Profound articulation adds to the making of genuinely places of refuge inside connections. At the point when people go ahead and express their sentiments unafraid of judgment or negation, trust and closeness flourish. Profound wellbeing empowers people to be defenseless, encouraging further associations and a conviction that all is good inside connections.

Empowering Development and Flexibility:

Through close to home articulation, people explore difficulties, misfortunes, and wins inside connections. Sharing both positive and testing feelings considers common help and consolation. The groundbreaking power lies in the aggregate development and strength that rises up out of exploring the close to home landscape together.

Social and Orientation Impacts on Profound Articulation:

The statement of feelings is impacted by social standards, cultural assumptions, and orientation jobs. Social settings shape the adequate manners by which feelings are communicated, and people might explore these standards while additionally communicating their genuine close to home encounters. Also, orientation generalizations frequently influence how feelings are seen and communicated, adding to one of a kind difficulties and assumptions.

Social Varieties:

Various societies might have unmistakable standards with respect to profound articulation. A few societies might support open presentations of feeling, while others might focus on close to home restriction. Exploring the social effects on close to home articulation includes understanding and regarding assorted ways to deal with sentiments inside unambiguous social settings.

Orientation Assumptions:

Cultural assumptions connected with orientation frequently impact how feelings are communicated and seen. Customary orientation standards might recommend specific close to home presentations as more adequate for one orientation over another. Exploring orientation assumptions includes testing generalizations, advancing close to home validness, and perceiving the variety of profound encounters across sexes.

Showing The ability to understand individuals on a profound level to Kids:

Developing capacity to understand individuals on a profound level since the beginning outfits youngsters with fundamental abilities for exploring the close to home landscape all through their lives. Guardians, parental figures, and teachers assume an essential part in showing the capacity to understand people at their core to kids through deliberate direction and job demonstrating.

Displaying Close to home Articulation:

Kids advance by noticing the profound articulations of grown-ups in their lives. Displaying solid close to home articulation includes straightforwardly sharing sentiments, examining profound encounters, and showing helpful ways of exploring testing feelings. This displaying makes an establishment for youngsters to foster their capacity to understand people on a deeper level.

Empowering Profound Jargon:

Creating the capacity to understand anyone on a deeper level incorporates extending one's close to home jargon.

Empowering youngsters to distinguish and explain their sentiments utilizing explicit words advances mindfulness and powerful correspondence. Making a place of refuge for youngsters to communicate many feelings cultivates profound education.

Showing Ways of dealing with hardship or stress:

The capacity to appreciate people on a deeper level includes the capacity to adapt to testing feelings in valuable ways. Showing kids survival methods, like profound breathing, care, and innovative articulation, gives them instruments for self-guideline. These techniques add to close to home strength and prosperity.

Advancing Sympathy and Viewpoint Taking:

Compassion is a critical part of the capacity to understand individuals on a deeper level. Advancing compassion includes helping youngsters comprehend and think about the sensations of others. Participating in exercises that empower point of view taking, for example, narrating or pretending, develops a feeling of sympathy and upgrades relational abilities.

Esteeming Close to home Variety:

Perceiving and esteeming the variety of profound encounters is basic to the capacity to understand anyone on a deeper level. Instructing youngsters that all feelings are substantial and that everybody encounters a scope of sentiments adds to a more comprehensive comprehension of feelings. This approach encourages acknowledgment and decreases disgrace encompassing specific feelings.

Flourishing in the Woven artwork of Feelings

Exploring the profound landscape is a progressing and dynamic excursion that unfurls over the course of life. Grasping the range of feelings, embracing profound articulation, and developing capacity to understand people on a deeper level add to a rich embroidery of human encounters. In perceiving the groundbreaking force of exploring feelings, people set out on an excursion of self-revelation, association, and self-improvement.

The intricacy of feelings highlights their significant effect on individual prosperity and the elements of connections. Embracing both the positive and testing parts of the close to home territory considers a more all encompassing comprehension of oneself as well as other people. Credible close to home articulation turns into a scaffold that interfaces people, cultivating further associations and shared human encounters.

As people explore the unpredictable scene of feelings, they become engineers of their profound prosperity, forming the nature of their connections and impacting the more extensive embroidered artwork of human association. The groundbreaking excursion inside the profound landscape is a persistent course of investigation, self-reflection, and the cognizant development of the capacity to understand individuals on a deeper level — an excursion that unfurls with the lavishness of the human experience.

5.1 Understanding the emotional landscape of childhood.

Grasping the Profound Scene of Experience growing up: Sustaining Close to home Prosperity and Versatility

The close to home scene of young life is a mind boggling and energetic territory, set apart by a heap of sentiments and encounters that shape a kid's identity, connections, and perspective. This investigation digs into the complexities of the close to home scene, stressing the meaning of cultivating profound prosperity and versatility during the early stages. From the essential job of early profound encounters to the effect of outer impacts, understanding the close to home scene is significant for guardians, parental figures, and teachers in supporting youngsters' all encompassing turn of events.

Underpinnings of Early Profound Encounters:

The seeds of profound prosperity are planted in the earliest snapshots of life, as babies and small kids start to explore the world from a perspective of feelings. The nature of early profound encounters, frequently molded by cooperations with guardians, sets the basis for a youngster's close to home scene. Connection, a central part of early close to home turn of events, assumes a crucial part in laying out a feeling of safety and trust.

Connection and Close to home Security:

Connection alludes to the close to home bond framed between a youngster and their essential parental figure. This bond is essential to a youngster's close to home security and establishes the groundwork for future connections. Secure connection, described by responsive and sincerely adjusted providing care, gives a feeling of safety that permits youngsters to investigate the world with certainty.

Alternately, shaky connection, coming about because of conflicting providing care or profound inaccessibility, can add to elevated feelings of anxiety and troubles in directing feelings. Understanding the effect of connection on the close to home scene highlights the significance of supporting secure associations in youth.

Profound Guideline Improvement:

Profound guideline, the capacity to oversee and tweak one's feelings, goes through huge improvement during youth. Babies and small kids depend on parental figures to assist with managing their feelings, progressively incorporating these administrative abilities after some time. The close to home scene of youth is set apart by the investigation of different feelings and the slow procurement of procedures for adapting to both good and testing sentiments.

Guardians and parental figures assume a focal part in supporting the improvement of close to home guideline by giving a responsive and encouraging presence. The capacity to calm a bothered kid, recognize their sentiments, and model sound profound articulation adds to the development of successful close to home guideline abilities.

Impact of Outer Variables on the Profound Scene:

While early encounters inside the nuclear family shape a huge piece of the profound scene, outer factors like companions, school, and cultural impacts additionally assume vital parts. The interchange between these outer components and the inward profound universe of a kid adds to the intricacy of their close to home encounters.

Peer Connections and Social Elements:

As kids change into young, peer connections become progressively persuasive in molding the close to home scene. Collaborations with peers add to the improvement of interactive abilities, sympathy, and the capacity to explore complex social elements. Good friend encounters cultivate a feeling of having a place and basic encouragement, while challenges in peer connections might summon sensations of dismissal or seclusion.

Understanding the effect of friend connections includes perceiving the job of socialization in forming a youngster's personal scene. Guardians and teachers assume pivotal parts in working with positive social associations, encouraging compassion, and giving direction on exploring the intricacies of friend elements.

Instructive Climate and Profound Learning:

The school climate is a critical field for profound turn of events, giving chances to learning, development, and socialization. Instructive settings add to the close to home scene by molding a kid's demeanor towards learning, confidence, and associations with power figures and friends.

Educators, as powerful figures in a youngster's life, assume a key part in making genuinely steady study halls. Rehearses that recognize and approve understudies' feelings, show close to home proficiency, and advance a good learning climate add to the profound prosperity of youngsters inside the instructive setting.

Media and Innovation Effect:

The unavoidable impact of media and innovation in contemporary society acquaints extra layers with the profound scene of life as a youngster. Openness to different types of media, including TV, motion pictures, and computerized stages, can shape a youngster's insights, values, and profound reactions.

Understanding the effect of media includes perceiving the potential for both positive and adverse impacts. Instructive substance can upgrade learning and advance positive qualities, while openness to unseemly or brutal material might add to tension or desensitization. Guardians and parental figures assume an essential part in directing kids' media utilization and working with discussions about the close to home substance experienced.

Articulation of Feelings in Youth:

The declaration of feelings is an essential part of the close to home scene, filling in as an essential means through which kids impart their inside states and needs. Empowering sound profound articulation includes establishing a strong climate that approves a kid's sentiments, gives outlets to innovative articulation, and encourages open correspondence.

The Job of Play in Close to home Articulation:

Play fills in as a characteristic road for kids to communicate and deal with their feelings. Play exercises, whether innovative, imaginative, or physical, permit youngsters to investigate a scope of sentiments in a protected and unstructured setting. Play additionally works with social and close to home learning, as kids participate in agreeable play, exchange, and the advancement of sympathy.

Guardians, parental figures, and teachers can uphold profound articulation through play by giving an assortment of play materials, empowering creative play situations, and partaking in play exercises that advance association and correspondence.

Inventive Expressions and Profound Correspondence:

The imaginative expressions, including drawing, painting, composing, and music, offer expressive source for youngsters to impart their feelings. Imaginative exercises give a nonverbal method for handling sentiments, encouraging self-reflection, and passing feelings that might be trying on to verbally expressive.

Coordinating imaginative expressions into a kid's standard considers the investigation of feelings in a restorative and charming way. Establishing a steady climate that values creative articulation adds to the close to home prosperity of kids and supports the improvement of a different profound jargon.

Empowering Verbal Articulation:

Verbal correspondence is a critical part of close to home articulation, permitting kids to express their sentiments, contemplations, and encounters. Empowering verbal articulation includes effectively paying attention to a youngster's words, giving space to them to share their feelings, and posing unconditional inquiries that advance self-reflection.

The advancement of verbal articulation is intently attached to language securing and education abilities. Guardians and teachers can uphold this part of profound articulation by taking part in significant discussions, perusing books that investigate feelings, and cultivating a language-rich climate that energizes correspondence.

Exploring Testing Feelings in Youth:

Youngsters, similar to grown-ups, experience a range of feelings, including those that might be seen as trying or troublesome. Exploring these feelings includes recognizing their presence, offering help, and furnishing kids with survival techniques to deal with the highs and lows of their profound scene.

Managing Tension:

Tension is a typical inclination experienced by kids, especially notwithstanding new encounters, scholarly tensions, or social difficulties. Exploring nervousness includes approving a kid's sentiments, giving consolation, and showing ways of dealing with stress like profound breathing, care, or perception methods.

Guardians and instructors can establish steady conditions that recognize the wellsprings of tension, advance a feeling of control, and support a development outlook that perspectives challenges as any open doors for learning and strength.

Tending to Outrage and Dissatisfaction:

Outrage and dissatisfaction are regular reactions to saw obstructions or neglected needs. Exploring these feelings includes assisting kids with figuring out the triggers for their indignation, helping solid ways of communicating and oversee dissatisfaction, and advancing critical thinking abilities.

Making spaces for helpful outlets, like actual work, craftsmanship, or journaling, permits kids to direct their energy in certain ways. Furthermore, displaying successful displeasure the executives procedures and giving steady direction add to the improvement of close to home guideline abilities.

Adapting to Bitterness and Misfortune:

Bitterness and sadness are feelings that kids might experience because of different encounters, including misfortune, advances, or changes in their current circumstance. Exploring these feelings includes recognizing the truth, setting out open doors for profound articulation, and offering solace and backing.

Guardians and parental figures assume an essential part in giving an encouraging presence, taking part in open discussions about sensations of misery, and working with exercises that advance recuperating and association. Making customs or remembrances can likewise add to the most common way of adapting to misfortune.

Building Close to home Flexibility in Adolescence:

Close to home strength is the capacity to return from difficulties, adjust to misfortune, and keep a positive feeling of prosperity. Encouraging profound versatility in youth includes sustaining a youngster's ability to adapt to misfortunes, foster a healthy identity viability, and develop an outlook that embraces learning and development.

Empowering a Development Mentality:

A development mentality, portrayed by the conviction that capacities and knowledge can be created through exertion and determination, adds to close to home flexibility. Empowering a development mentality includes lauding exertion, outlining difficulties as any open doors for learning, and stressing the worth of determination.

Guardians and teachers assume crucial parts in molding a youngster's outlook by giving uplifting feedback to exertion, reevaluating disappointments as growth opportunities, and encouraging a climate that values constant improvement.

Showing Critical thinking Abilities:

Critical thinking abilities are fundamental for exploring difficulties and mishaps. Showing kids how to move toward issues deliberately, separate them into sensible advances, and consider different arrangements adds to their profound versatility.

Guardians and teachers can uphold the advancement of critical thinking abilities by including kids in dynamic cycles, empowering independence, and giving direction on assessing expected arrangements and their outcomes.

Advancing Social Encouraging groups of people:

Social help is an essential calculate building close to home flexibility. Solid associations with family, companions, and steady grown-ups make an underpinning of profound prosperity. Advancing social help includes working with positive connections, showing relational abilities, and encouraging a feeling of having a place.

Guardians, parental figures, and teachers can assume dynamic parts in establishing conditions that support positive social cooperations, giving chances to peer associations, and displaying solid relationship elements.

Developing Care Practices:

Care works on, including profound breathing, reflection, and mindfulness works out, add to close to home flexibility by advancing self-guideline and stress decrease. Developing care includes incorporating these practices into a youngster's daily schedule and displaying them as survival techniques.

Guardians and teachers can present care rehearses through age-fitting exercises, for example, directed unwinding works out, careful breathing games, or nature strolls. These practices offer youngsters instruments for focusing themselves and exploring personal difficulties.

Social and Variety Contemplations in the Profound Scene:

The close to home scene of experience growing up is impacted by social standards, family customs, and various points of view on feelings. Perceiving and regarding social contrasts in close to home articulation is fundamental for understanding and supporting the profound prosperity of youngsters from different foundations.

Social Varieties in Close to home Articulation:

Various societies might have particular standards with respect to close to home articulation. A few societies might empower open presentations of warmth and feeling, while others might focus on profound limitation. Exploring social varieties includes regarding different ways to deal with close to home articulation and understanding the social setting in which a youngster is raised.

Family and Social Practices:

Family and social practices add to the close to home scene by molding the manners by which feelings are commended, communicated, or celebrated. Understanding the meaning of social customs includes perceiving the job they play in supporting qualities, encouraging a feeling of character, and giving a structure to close to home articulation.

Guardians, parental figures, and teachers can take part in open discussions about social practices, integrate assorted viewpoints into instructive educational plans, and establish comprehensive conditions that commend the wealth of social variety.

Bilingualism and Multilingualism:

Language is a crucial part of profound articulation, and kids experiencing childhood in bilingual or multilingual conditions explore the close to home scene through various etymological focal points. Bilingualism and multilingualism add to the lavishness of a kid's personal jargon and social character.

Supporting language improvement in different phonetic conditions includes perceiving the worth of every language, giving open doors to language upkeep, and cultivating a comprehensive climate that embraces semantic variety.

Supporting Strong and Sincerely Balanced Kids:

Understanding the profound scene of young life is a dynamic and multi-layered venture that requires a comprehensive methodology from guardians, parental figures, and teachers. From the central job of early profound encounters to the effect of outside impacts, the close to home scene shapes the direction of a kid's turn of events.

Sustaining close to home prosperity in youngsters includes perceiving the significance of secure connections, supporting solid profound articulation, and giving direction in exploring the intricacies of feelings.

By recognizing the impact of outer elements, like friend connections, instructive conditions, and social elements, grown-ups can make strong structures that add to a kid's personal strength.

Empowering the improvement of the capacity to appreciate people on a profound level, including the capacity to direct feelings, express them really, and relate to other people, outfits kids with fundamental abilities for deep rooted prosperity. Exploring testing feelings, building profound strength, and considering social and variety contemplations add to an exhaustive comprehension of the close to home scene.

As designers of kids' close to home scenes, guardians, parental figures, and teachers assume urgent parts in establishing conditions that cultivate development, versatility, and a positive identity. By embracing the complexities of the close to home excursion, grown-ups can add to the advancement of genuinely composed, sympathetic, and strong people who explore the intricacies of the world with certainty and empathy.

5.2 Addressing the challenges of recognizing and responding to emotional cues.

Addressing the Difficulties of Perceiving and Answering Profound Prompts: Exploring the Complexities of Close to home Correspondence

Exploring the unpredictable scene of close to home prompts presents novel difficulties, expecting people to interpret unpretentious signals and answer with compassion and attunement. Perceiving and answering close to home signs is principal for building significant associations, whether in private connections, proficient settings, or inside the nuclear family. This investigation digs into the intricacies of close to home correspondence, tending to the difficulties people face in precisely seeing and really answering the horde of signals that shape human connections.

The Intricacy of Close to home Prompts:

Close to home prompts incorporate an expansive range of non-verbal and verbal signs that convey a person's interior close to home states. From looks and non-verbal communication to manner of speaking and selection of words, these signals structure a complex language that frequently imparts more than words alone. The test lies in translating this nuanced correspondence, as profound signals can be unpretentious, setting subordinate, and affected by social and individual variables.

Non-Verbal Prompts:

Non-verbal prompts, like looks, motions, and stance, assume a huge part in conveying feelings. Be that as it may, deciphering these prompts precisely expects aversion to social varieties, individual contrasts, and the setting where they happen. A look that means satisfaction in one social setting might convey an alternate feeling in another, featuring the intricacy of non-verbal correspondence.

Verbal Prompts:

Verbal prompts incorporate the manner of speaking, selection of words, and the general correspondence style. The test in deciphering verbal signals emerges from the likely misalignment between expressed words and the hidden profound tone. For example, an individual might say they are fine, yet their manner of speaking and non-verbal prompts might recommend in any case. Exploring this incongruence requires sharp perception and attunement to the nuances of verbal articulation.

Social and Individual Varieties:

Social standards and individual contrasts add to the variety of close to home articulation. What might be viewed as a proper presentation of feelings in one social setting may be seen contrastingly in another. Also, individual character qualities and correspondence styles impact how close to home prompts are communicated and deciphered. Perceiving and regarding these varieties is pivotal for exact profound comprehension.

Challenges in Perceiving Close to home Signals:

While profound prompts are unavoidable in human correspondence, a few difficulties obstruct the precise acknowledgment of these signs. These difficulties come from both inner and outside factors, expecting people to explore mental inclinations, close to home guideline, and the effect of outer stressors.

Mental Predispositions:

Mental predispositions, for example, tendency to look for predetermined feedback and generalizing, can impact how people see and decipher close to home signals. Assumptions or generalizations about an individual or circumstance might cloud one's capacity to precisely perceive the feelings being conveyed. Beating mental inclinations includes developing mindfulness, embracing an open outlook, and testing programmed suspicions.

Profound Guideline:

The capacity to precisely perceive close to home signs is unpredictably connected to one's own personal guideline. People who battle to deal with their own feelings might find it trying to adjust to the feelings of others. Profound guideline includes mindfulness, the capacity to adapt to individual sentiments, and a limit with respect to compassionate comprehension. Fostering these abilities improves the exactness of perceiving profound signs.

Outside Stressors:

Outside stressors, like time imperatives, natural interruptions, or individual pressure, can block the mindful acknowledgment of close to home prompts. In speedy or high-pressure circumstances, people might focus on effectiveness over profound attunement, prompting possible misconceptions. Moderating the effect of outer stressors includes establishing conditions helpful for centered correspondence and cultivating care in relational associations.

Equivocalness and Contradicting messages:

Profound correspondence is intrinsically nuanced, and circumstances frequently present contradicting messages or vague signals. An individual might show clashing non-verbal and verbal signals, making it trying to perceive their actual profound state. Exploring uncertainty requires a nuanced comprehension of meaningful gestures, undivided attention abilities, and the readiness to look for explanation when confronted with inconsistent messages.

Hindrances to Compelling Reaction:

Perceiving profound signs is just the initial step; answering actually is similarly basic for cultivating significant associations. Different hindrances can thwart the capacity to answer properly to profound signals, going from an absence of compassion to correspondence boundaries and the anxiety toward weakness.

Absence of Sympathy:

Sympathy is the foundation of compelling close to home responsiveness. An absence of sympathy, whether because of individual elements or profound exhaustion, can block the capacity to answer with understanding and empathy. Developing sympathy includes effectively tuning in, context taking, and cultivating a certified interest in others' close to home encounters.

Correspondence Obstructions:

Correspondence obstructions, like poor verbal abilities, an absence of confidence, or trouble communicating feelings, can block the capacity to answer successfully to close to home prompts. Conquering these obstructions includes creating relational abilities, including undivided attention, confident articulation, and the ability to express sentiments and reactions with clearness.

Feeling of dread toward Weakness:

Answering really to close to home prompts requires a level of weakness, as it includes sharing one's own feelings and interfacing on a more profound level. Feeling of dread toward weakness can appear as protectiveness, evasion, or a hesitance to participate in sincerely charged discussions. Beating this dread includes establishing a protected and believing climate that supports open articulation and profound sharing.

Confused Correspondence Styles:

People might have different correspondence styles, and a confuse between styles can make hindrances to viable reaction. For instance, an individual who favors direct correspondence might find it trying to interface with somebody who imparts all the more by implication. Spanning these holes includes versatility, undivided attention, and an eagerness to comprehend and oblige different correspondence styles.

Procedures for Improving Close to home Mindfulness and Responsiveness:

Conquering the difficulties of perceiving and answering close to home signals requires purposeful endeavors to improve profound mindfulness, foster sympathetic abilities, and establish conditions helpful for open correspondence. A few techniques can add to this interaction:

Careful Presence:

Developing careful presence includes being completely present at the time and effectively took part in the correspondence cycle. Care rehearses, like profound breathing or establishing works out, can upgrade mindfulness and attunement to close to home signals. Integrating care into day to day schedules encourages an elevated condition of mindfulness in relational connections.

Undivided attention:

Undivided attention is a principal expertise for perceiving and answering profound signs. It includes focusing on the speaker, rewording to affirm understanding, and giving input that reflects sympathy. Undivided attention makes a space for people to communicate their feelings transparently, adding to a more significant association.

Sympathy Advancement:

Sympathy is a powerful expertise that can be created through deliberate practice. Participating in context taking activities, perusing writing that investigates assorted profound encounters, and effectively trying to comprehend others' perspectives add to compassion improvement. Sympathy frames the establishment for genuine and caring reactions to profound signs.

Close to home Guideline Practices:

Improving profound guideline abilities is critical for both perceiving and answering close to home prompts really. Practices like self-reflection, care contemplation, and journaling add to mindfulness and profound guideline. By getting it and overseeing individual feelings, people are better outfitted to connect sympathetically with the feelings of others.

Social Capability Preparing:

Given the impact of social minor departure from close to home articulation, social skill preparing can upgrade one's capacity to explore different profound scenes. This preparing includes finding out about various social standards, testing generalizations, and creating aversion to the effect of social variables on close to home correspondence.

Relational abilities Advancement:

Creating successful relational abilities is fundamental for defeating hindrances to both acknowledgment and reaction.

This incorporates decisiveness preparing, figuring out how to communicate feelings obviously and consciously, and leveling up the skill to adjust correspondence styles to various relational elements. Relational abilities enable people to explore complex profound collaborations with certainty.

Making Places of refuge:

Laying out protected and believing conditions is basic for open profound correspondence. Making spaces where people feel open to communicating their feelings unafraid of judgment encourages a culture of legitimacy. This includes advancing mental security, effectively tuning in without judgment, and approving the feelings of others.

Building The capacity to appreciate people on a profound level:

Building the capacity to appreciate anyone on a deeper level includes improving the skill to perceive, comprehend, and oversee both individual and others' feelings. Instructive projects and studios on capacity to appreciate people at their core can give important experiences and abilities to exploring close to home signals in different settings. By outfitting people with the devices of the capacity to understand individuals on a profound level, society can encourage more sympathetic and responsive relational elements.

The Craftsmanship and Study of Profound Correspondence

Perceiving and answering profound prompts is both a workmanship and a science, requiring a fragile equilibrium of sympathy, mindfulness, and compelling correspondence. The difficulties innate in disentangling the intricacies of close to home articulation highlight the requirement for deliberate endeavors to improve the ability to appreciate people on a deeper level and encourage compassionate responsiveness.

As people explore the complexities of close to home correspondence, they add to the formation of additional merciful and figuring out networks. By recognizing the variety of profound articulations, embracing social capability, and developing compassionate associations, society can move towards an additional genuinely insightful and responsive group.

At last, the excursion of perceiving and answering profound signals is a deep rooted course of learning, self-revelation, and nonstop development. Through deliberate practices, schooling, and the advancement of sympathetic correspondence, people can explore the mind boggling scene of feelings with effortlessness, cultivating associations that add to the extravagance of the human experience.

5.3 Practical tips for fostering emotional intelligence in children.

Pragmatic Ways to cultivate The ability to understand anyone on a profound level in Youngsters: Sustaining the Establishments for Deep rooted Prosperity

Encouraging capacity to understand people on a deeper level in youngsters is a basic part of their comprehensive turn of events. The capacity to appreciate people on a profound level envelops the capacity to perceive, comprehend, make due, and express feelings successfully, both in oneself as well as other people. Building this vital ability furnishes youngsters with the devices expected to explore complex social cooperations, assemble positive connections, and upgrade in general prosperity. This investigation dives into down to earth tips for guardians, parental figures, and teachers to support the capacity to understand people on a deeper level in youngsters, laying the foundation for a versatile and genuinely mindful future.

1. Develop a Protected and Open Climate:
   The establishment for creating the capacity to understand individuals on a profound level starts with establishing a protected and open climate where kids feel open to communicating their feelings unafraid of judgment or discipline. Energize open correspondence, effectively pay attention to their sentiments, and approve their close to home encounters. A place of refuge permits youngsters to investigate and figure out their feelings, cultivating mindfulness.

2. Model Ability to appreciate individuals on a deeper level:
   Kids advance by noticing the way of behaving of the huge grown-ups in their lives. Displaying the ability to appreciate individuals at their core includes exhibiting solid approaches to communicating and dealing with feelings. Exhibit mindfulness by recognizing your sentiments, express feelings in a suitable way, and feature critical thinking techniques when confronted with difficulties. Demonstrating furnishes youngsters with unmistakable instances of the capacity to understand anyone on a profound level in real life.

3. Show Close to home Jargon:
   Building the capacity to understand people at their core requires a vigorous profound jargon. Show youngsters a different scope of feeling words to help them articulate and recognize their sentiments precisely. Talk about feelings in regular circumstances, read books that investigate different sentiments, and urge them to communicate how they feel in various situations. Fostering a rich profound jargon improves their capacity to impart and figure out feelings.

4. Support Compassion:
   Compassion is a critical part of the capacity to appreciate people on a profound level, empowering people to comprehend and discuss the thoughts of others. Cultivate sympathy in kids by empowering point of view taking exercises, talking about the feelings of story

characters, and aiding them perceive and approve the sensations of their companions.

By understanding others' viewpoints, kids foster more grounded relational abilities and a more profound association with their friends.

5. **Give Apparatuses to Profound Guideline:**
   Profound guideline is a basic part of the capacity to understand individuals on a deeper level. Outfit kids with viable apparatuses and systems to manage their feelings when confronted with difficulties. This might incorporate profound breathing activities, care exercises, or basic methods like building up to ten. Training kids to deal with their profound reactions enables them to explore different circumstances with strength.

6. **Cultivate Critical thinking Abilities:**
   Critical thinking is a fundamental piece of the ability to appreciate individuals on a profound level, as it includes tracking down useful answers for difficulties. Urge youngsters to contemplate issues, think about elective arrangements, and pursue choices that line up with their qualities. Including them in dynamic cycles cultivates a feeling of independence and supports the connection between the capacity to understand people on a profound level and powerful critical thinking.

7. **Support Sound Gamble Taking:**
   Urge kids to step outside their usual ranges of familiarity and face solid challenges. Whether it's difficult another movement, making new companions, or taking part in bunch exercises, exploring these encounters helps assemble profound flexibility. Recognize their endeavors, no matter what the result, and underscore the benefit of learning and development through new encounters.

8. **Consolidate Close to home Learning in Schooling:**
   Coordinate profound learning into the instructive educational program to underscore the significance of the capacity to understand anyone on a deeper level. Make illustrations and exercises that investigate feelings, connections, and compromise. Giving an organized system to profound learning assists youngsters with grasping the meaning of feelings in different settings, cultivating a more thorough way to deal with their schooling.

9. **Advance Intelligent Practices:**
   Develop a propensity for appearance in kids by empowering them to ponder their feelings and encounters. This should be possible through journaling, narrating, or unassuming conversations. Intelligent practices assist youngsters with making associations between

their feelings, activities, and the outcomes of their decisions, adding to the advancement of mindfulness.

10. Energize Positive Social Cooperations:
    Social collaborations give an important field to rehearsing the capacity to understand individuals on a deeper level.
    Empower positive social communications, participation, and cooperation. Show kids compelling relational abilities, compromise techniques, and the significance of compassion in building solid and sound connections.

11. Embrace Profound Variety:
    Assist youngsters with understanding that all feelings are legitimate and part of the human experience. Embrace profound variety by examining many feelings, recognizing that feeling a range of feelings is ordinary. This cultivates a comprehensive comprehension of feelings and decreases disgrace encompassing specific sentiments, empowering kids to really communicate their thoughts.

12. Set Practical Assumptions:
    Laying out practical assumptions for kids' personal improvement is essential. Perceive that every youngster is interesting, and the capacity to appreciate individuals on a profound level creates at various rates. Abstain from forcing unreasonable assumptions or excusing their feelings. Celebrate little triumphs, energize progress, and offer help during testing minutes.

13. Advance a Development Mentality:
    Develop a development mentality by underscoring the worth of exertion, learning, and versatility. Instruct youngsters that difficulties are open doors for development and that insight, including the capacity to understand anyone on a deeper level, can be created through devotion and constancy. Cultivating a development outlook ingrains an uplifting perspective towards learning and adjusting to new profound encounters.

14. Work with Imaginative Articulation:
    Imaginative outlets, like drawing, painting, and different types of creative articulation, furnish kids with elective ways of imparting and interaction their feelings. Urge them to articulate their thoughts through workmanship, considering a non-verbal investigation of their sentiments. Imaginative articulation cultivates innovativeness and profound delivery.

15. Be Patient and Steady:

Creating the capacity to understand people on a profound level is a progressive cycle, and kids might confront difficulties en route. Show restraint, strong, and understanding. Make an air where they have a real sense of reassurance to commit errors, gain from encounters, and develop inwardly. Praise their advancement and give consolation during snapshots of trouble.

Sustaining Deep rooted Profound Prosperity

Encouraging capacity to understand people on a profound level in kids is a dynamic and progressing process that requires purposeful endeavors from guardians, parental figures, and teachers.

By establishing conditions that focus on close to home prosperity, demonstrating sound profound ways of behaving, and consolidating pragmatic techniques for the ability to appreciate anyone on a deeper level turn of events, grown-ups assume vital parts in molding the profound scene of the future.

Sustaining the capacity to understand people on a deeper level lays the preparation for a long period of prosperity, flexibility, and positive social connections. As youngsters foster the abilities to perceive, comprehend, and explore their feelings, they improve their own emotional wellness as well as add to the production of sympathetic and genuinely insightful networks. Through insightful direction and backing, grown-ups enable youngsters to set out on an excursion of self-revelation, relational association, and deep rooted profound development.

Chapter 6

Lost in Translation

The complexities of multifaceted correspondence present a maze of difficulties, where subtleties, nuances, and different viewpoints join, frequently prompting misconceptions or misinterpretations. The expression "Lost in Interpretation" typifies the intricacy of conveying significance across various social settings, underlining the hardships that emerge when people from unmistakable social foundations participate in correspondence. This investigation digs into the diverse layers of multifaceted correspondence, disentangling the variables that add to miscommunication, and offering bits of knowledge into cultivating social skill and compelling worldwide discourse.

Social Groundworks of Correspondence:

Correspondence isn't simply the transmission of words; profoundly implanted in social systems shape language, articulations, and translation. Culture incorporates a range of components, including values, convictions, standards, and social designs, impacting how people see and convey meaning. At the point when people from assorted societies meet up, they carry with them novel social focal points through which they decipher verbal and non-verbal prompts.

Language Subtleties:

Language, as an essential vehicle of correspondence, conveys social subtleties that reach out past exacting interpretations. Phrases, everyday articulations, and social references might hold various implications in assorted phonetic scenes.

At the point when people impart in a language that isn't their local tongue, the gamble of misjudging or missing unobtrusive social prompts enhances, adding to the peculiarity of being "Lost in Interpretation."

Non-Verbal Correspondence:

Non-verbal prompts, like non-verbal communication, looks, and motions, are strong communicators profoundly imbued in social settings. Notwithstanding, the understanding of these signs changes across societies. What might be viewed as a noble gesture in one culture could be seen as decisiveness or even impoliteness in another. Understanding the social components of non-verbal correspondence is fundamental for exploring culturally diverse communications.

Obstructions to Multifaceted Correspondence:

The excursion of multifaceted correspondence is loaded with hindrances that prevent viable comprehension. These hindrances are established in contrasts in correspondence styles, perspectives, and assumptions, and they manifest in different structures, frequently prompting potentially negative side-effects.

Generalizations and Biases:

Generalizations and biases about a specific culture can shape assumptions and impact understandings. At the point when people depend on generalizations as opposed to trying to comprehend the exceptional viewpoints of others, miscommunication becomes unavoidable. Defeating these predispositions requires a cognizant work to move toward multifaceted collaborations with a receptive outlook and an eagerness to learn.

Social Relativism:

Social relativism, the propensity to assess and pass judgment on one more culture in view of one's own social norms, can make critical hindrances. At the point when people neglect to perceive and regard social contrasts, misinterpretations emerge. Embracing social relativism includes recognizing that different social practices are legitimate inside their individual settings and not review them from a perspective of ethnocentrism.

High-Setting versus Low-Setting Correspondence:

Societies change in their correspondence styles, with some being high-setting and others low-setting. High-setting societies depend intensely on certain correspondence, where a lot is passed on through setting, tone, and non-verbal signals. Interestingly, low-setting societies focus on express verbal correspondence. At the point when people from these differentiating societies cooperate, the potential for errors emerges due to contrasting assumptions about how data is conveyed and deciphered.

Power Distance:

Power distance, the degree to which people in a general public acknowledge progressive contrasts, impacts correspondence elements. In high power distance societies, people might be more held in communicating contradiction or conflict with power figures. In low power distance societies, correspondence will in general be more libertarian. Arranging these power elements is vital for compelling culturally diverse correspondence, as misalignments in assumptions might prompt misinterpretations.

Independence versus Cooperation:

The social components of independence and cooperation influence how people focus on private objectives versus bunch amicability. In individualistic societies, direct correspondence and decisiveness might be esteemed, while in collectivistic societies, backhanded correspondence and concordance safeguarding are underscored. Perceiving these social directions is fundamental for exploring assumptions and staying away from expected clashes.

Techniques for Compelling Culturally diverse Correspondence:

Exploring the difficulties of multifaceted correspondence requires a proactive methodology that embraces social variety, cultivates understanding, and empowers versatility. Utilizing systems that advance successful correspondence across social limits is fundamental for building extensions and cultivating worldwide comprehension.

Social Responsiveness Preparing:

Furnishing people with social responsiveness preparing outfits them with the information and abilities expected to explore diverse cooperations. Preparing projects can cover social mindfulness, correspondence styles, and explicit social subtleties to upgrade members' comprehension and responsiveness in assorted settings.

Undivided attention:

Undivided attention is a general correspondence expertise that takes on uplifted importance in diverse settings. Effectively paying attention to the viewpoints, concerns, and articulations of people from various societies shows regard and a certified interest in understanding. It includes hearing words as well as focusing on non-verbal signals and the social setting encompassing the correspondence.

Social Insight (CQ):

Social knowledge, or CQ, alludes to a singular's ability to work actually in socially different settings. Creating CQ includes improving social information, building social care, and leveling up relational abilities across societies. People with high CQ are better prepared to adjust to new social conditions and explore diverse correspondence with responsiveness.

Explain and Affirm Understanding:

Uncertainty is a typical test in multifaceted correspondence. To alleviate false impressions, people ought to explain and affirm how they might interpret data traded.

This might include rewording, summing up, or posing unassuming inquiries to guarantee that the two players share a typical comprehension of the imparted message.

Embrace Variety in Correspondence Styles:
Societies show different correspondence styles, going from immediate and emphatic to backhanded and nuanced. Embracing this variety includes perceiving that there is nobody size-fits-all way to deal with correspondence. Adaptability and versatility in changing one's correspondence style to line up with social inclinations add to additional powerful diverse connections.

Foster Relational Connections:
Building relational connections across societies cultivates trust and upgrades correspondence. Finding opportunity to figure out the social foundation of partners, companions, or accomplices lays out a groundwork of regard and appreciation. Special interactions frequently act as scaffolds, permitting people to really explore social contrasts more.

Advance Comprehensive Language:
Language decisions can fundamentally influence diverse correspondence. Utilizing comprehensive language that evades social predisposition or preference adds to establishing a climate of correspondence and regard. This includes being aware of likely social responsive qualities and picking words that are comprehensive and all around comprehended.

Look for Input:
Effectively looking for input from people of various social foundations gives important bits of knowledge into the adequacy of correspondence. This input circle takes into account consistent improvement and changes in accordance with correspondence systems. Establishing a climate where input is invited supports open exchange and shared understanding.

Lay out Shared view:
Figuring out some mutual interest cultivates a feeling of common perspective and association. Recognizing normal qualities, objectives, or interests makes an establishment for successful correspondence. Laying out shared conviction helps span social holes and advances joint effort and participation.

Multifaceted Joint effort:
Effectively captivating in multifaceted joint effort, whether through work projects, local area drives, or instructive projects, gives useful involvement with exploring social contrasts. Cooperative endeavors set out open doors for getting the hang of, encouraging a feeling of common regard and understanding.

The Job of Innovation in Diverse Correspondence:
In a period of worldwide network, innovation assumes a crucial part in working with culturally diverse correspondence. Advanced stages, video conferencing, and texting give roads to people from various areas of the

planet to associate. In any case, utilizing innovation for powerful multifaceted correspondence requires careful contemplations:

Language Interpretation Instruments:

Language interpretation apparatuses can support beating language hindrances by giving constant interpretation of composed or spoken content. While these apparatuses are important, they may not catch social subtleties precisely. People ought to utilize them sensibly and know about possible limits.

Video Conferencing Behavior:

Video conferencing has turned into a staple in diverse correspondence. Understanding and regarding video conferencing decorum, including social standards connected with clothing, good tidings, and support, adds to a positive virtual correspondence experience.

Social Responsiveness in Virtual Stages:

Virtual stages ought to focus on social responsiveness in their plan and highlights. Highlights that take into consideration customization in light of social inclinations, different language choices, and familiarity with social subtleties add to a more comprehensive and powerful virtual correspondence climate.

Computerized Culturally diverse Preparation:

Computerized stages can have culturally diverse preparation modules, online classes, or studios that people can get to from a distance. These computerized assets give adaptability in finding out about social contrasts and successful correspondence methodologies, taking care of a worldwide crowd looking to upgrade their diverse capability.

Exploring the Worldwide Embroidery of Correspondence

The difficulties innate in multifaceted correspondence highlight the requirement for people to foster social capability — a range of abilities that goes past language capability to envelop a comprehension of different social standards, values, and correspondence styles. Being "Lost in Interpretation" isn't a certainty yet rather a source of inspiration for people to effectively take part in the excursion of grasping, learning, and spanning social partitions.

Compelling multifaceted correspondence is a continuous interaction that requires ceaseless learning and transformation. As people endeavor to improve their social knowledge, embrace variety, and develop receptiveness, they add to the production of a worldwide embroidery of correspondence that is wealthy in figuring out, regard, and shared importance.

By cultivating a culture of inclusivity and esteeming the exceptional viewpoints that each culture brings, we can change the difficulties of diverse correspondence into open doors for association, coordinated effort, and shared improvement.

6.1 Investigating common misinterpretations of children's behaviors.

Understanding the multifaceted language of experience growing up conduct is likened to unraveling an intricate embroidery woven with strings of feelings, necessities, and one of a kind singularity. Youngsters impart their contemplations and sentiments through activities, articulations, and cooperations with their general surroundings. Nonetheless, the test lies in deciphering these ways of behaving precisely, as grown-ups may unexpectedly misread or misconstrue the unobtrusive signs youngsters discharge. This investigation dives into the normal misinterpretations of kids' ways of behaving, revealing insight into the nuanced idea of life as a youngster articulation and offering bits of knowledge into encouraging more precise comprehension and responsive providing care.

1. **Fits and Profound Explosions:**
   One of the most widely recognized misinterpretations includes fits and profound eruptions. Grown-ups may see these extraordinary presentations of feeling as simple consideration chasing or manipulative way of behaving. Be that as it may, fits frequently act as a specialized instrument for small kids who might come up short on verbal abilities to really communicate their necessities or dissatisfactions. Instead of excusing fits of rage, grown-ups ought to see them as signs of neglected needs or overpowering feelings, inciting investigation into the main driver and offering proper help.

2. **Withdrawal and Quiet:**
   At the point when kids pull out or become quiet, grown-ups could misconstrue this way of behaving as rebellion, touchiness, or an absence of commitment. Nonetheless, such withdrawal can be a survival strategy, flagging that a kid is handling feelings, feeling overpowered, or wrestling with subtle conflicts. Confounding quietness as lack of engagement might prompt an absence of steady mediation when, as a matter of fact, the youngster might profit from delicate support, a place of refuge to share, and consolation.

3. **Hostility and Resistance:**
   Forceful way of behaving and insubordination are much of the time misjudged as deliberate rebellion or an indication of a "troublesome" youngster. As a general rule, these ways of behaving may rise up out of neglected needs, dissatisfaction, or a longing for independence. Confounding hostility as resolute noncompliance can prompt correctional measures, while a more sympathetic methodology includes uncovering the hidden causes, showing elective ways of dealing with hardship or stress, and addressing the underlying problems adding to the youngster's difficult way of behaving.

4. Tenacity and Reliance:
   Kids displaying tenacity or reliance may be seen as excessively connected or "ruined." Be that as it may, such way of behaving frequently comes from a kid's requirement for security, consolation, or a reaction to a massive change or stressor. Misconstruing tenacity might result in unintentionally driving the kid away, while a steady methodology includes giving profound consolation, steadily reassuring freedom, and recognizing the kid's requirement for association.

5. Protection from Changes:
   Protection from changes, like leaving a play region or progressing between exercises, is a typical way of behaving that can be confused as hardheadedness. Instead of survey it exclusively as insubordination, perceiving that kids frequently battle with changes because of a requirement for consistency and control can illuminate a more sympathetic reaction. Offering clear correspondence, admonitions about forthcoming changes, and including kids in the dynamic cycle can moderate obstruction.

6. Overactivity and Fretfulness:
   Overactive or fretful way of behaving might be mistakenly seen as hyperactivity or an absence of discipline. While consideration related concerns exist, confounding hyperactivity disregarding ecological elements, tangible necessities, or age-suitable energy levels can prompt pointless naming. Tending to overactivity requires a comprehensive methodology, taking into account active work, routine changes, and distinguishing potential hidden factors adding to fretfulness.

7. Particular Mutism:
   Particular mutism, where a youngster reliably doesn't talk in unambiguous social circumstances, can be confounded as bashfulness or conscious refusal to convey. Nonetheless, specific mutism frequently originates from tension and a failure to beat hindrances in specific settings. Confounding this conduct might bring about expanded strain on the kid, compounding uneasiness. A strong methodology includes progressive openness, building trust, and encouraging an agreeable, harmless climate for correspondence.

8. Hairsplitting:
   Kids showing perfectionistic propensities might be seen as successful people, yet misconstruing this way of behaving disregarding the close to home cost can be adverse. Hairsplitting might be driven by dread of disappointment, nervousness, or a requirement for endorsement. Misconstruing hairsplitting as a positive characteristic may unintentionally add to pressure and tension. Empowering a

reasonable way to deal with difficulties, commending exertion over results, and cultivating versatility can assist youngsters with overseeing perfectionistic inclinations.

9. **Staring off into space or Distractibility:**

   Kids who dream or show up quickly drawn offtrack might be misjudged as unengaged or unmindful. In any case, these ways of behaving can be characteristic of different elements, including imagination, fatigue, or attentional difficulties.

   Misjudging distractibility might prompt disappointment or marking without tending to the fundamental causes. Understanding the specific circumstance, recognizing individual learning styles, and giving drawing in exercises can uphold kids who show fantasizing or distractibility.

10. **Relapse in Conduct:**

    Relapse, for example, bedwetting, thumb-sucking, or tenacity, may be misconstrued as a conscious re-visitation of "immature" conduct. Be that as it may, relapse frequently happens in light of pressure, advances, or personal difficulties. Confounding relapse as consideration looking for may bring about reformatory measures, while a steady reaction includes recognizing the kid's close to home state, giving consolation, and tending to the fundamental stressors.

11. **Fanciful Mates or Dream Play:**

    Kids participating in creative play or making fanciful friends might be misjudged as looking for consideration or taking part in deceptions. Notwithstanding, these exercises are an ordinary piece of mental turn of events, cultivating innovativeness, and close to home articulation. Misjudging dream play might prompt putting inventive exercises, neglecting their formative advantages down. Empowering imaginative articulation, partaking in dream play, and recognizing the youngster's rich creative mind can support this part of experience growing up advancement.

12. **Protection from Power:**

Protection from power figures, like instructors or guardians, might be misconstrued as rebellion or discourtesy. Nonetheless, this conduct can result from a craving for independence, a requirement for more clear correspondence, or moves in adjusting to power structures. Misconstruing opposition might prompt disciplinary measures, while resolving the fundamental issues includes open correspondence, setting clear assumptions, and giving open doors to independence inside limits.

Exploring Misinterpretations:

Understanding and tending to normal misinterpretations of youngsters' ways of behaving require a nuanced and compassionate methodology. By perceiving the complex idea of life as a youngster articulation, grown-ups can establish steady conditions that cultivate sound turn of events and successful correspondence. A few procedures can support exploring and relieving misinterpretations:

Develop Sympathy:

Developing sympathy includes effectively trying to grasp a youngster's viewpoint, recognizing their feelings, and perceiving the legitimacy of their encounters. By putting oneself from the kid's perspective, grown-ups can foster a more profound comprehension of the inspirations driving specific ways of behaving and answer with empathy.

Correspondence Transparently:

Transparent correspondence is critical in disentangling misinterpretations. Empowering kids to offer their viewpoints and sentiments, regardless of whether non-verbal, gives bits of knowledge into their reality. Grown-ups ought to likewise impart transparently about their perceptions, looking for explanation when ways of behaving are hazy and cultivating a climate where kids have a solid sense of security to share.

Think about Formative Stages:

Perceiving age-suitable ways of behaving and taking into account formative stages is fundamental in keeping away from misinterpretations. Kids go through different phases of development, each joined by unmistakable ways of behaving and challenges. Adjusting assumptions to formative achievements helps in grasping the setting of ways of behaving and answering suitably.

Fabricate Confiding in Connections:

Trust is central in translating youngsters' ways of behaving precisely. Building believing connections includes steady help, unwavering quality, and a non-critical methodology. Kids are bound to put themselves out there truly when they have a solid sense of safety and grasped, lessening the probability of misinterpretations.

Team up with Parental figures:

Cooperation between guardians, parental figures, and teachers is fundamental in tending to misinterpretations reliably. Sharing perceptions, experiences, and concerns takes into consideration a comprehensive comprehension of the kid's way of behaving. Cooperative endeavors guarantee that reactions are adjusted, giving a brought together and strong way to deal with kids' requirements.

Look for Proficient Direction:

At the point when ways of behaving raise concerns or endure, looking for proficient direction from teachers, pediatricians, or youngster clinicians can give significant experiences. Experts can direct appraisals, offer direction on formative achievements, and recognize any hidden difficulties that might add to specific ways of behaving.

Teach Grown-ups on Youngster Advancement:

Training on youngster improvement furnishes grown-ups with a thorough comprehension old enough proper ways of behaving and formative stages. Preparing projects, studios, or assets that attention on youngster brain science and conduct can upgrade grown-ups' capacity to precisely decipher and answer kids' prompts.

Energize Observational Abilities:

Creating sharp observational abilities empowers grown-ups to see unpretentious signs and changes in youngsters' ways of behaving. Effectively noticing non-verbal communication, looks, and collaborations gives significant data to grasping kids' close to home states and tending to any likely misinterpretations.

Give an Assortment of Correspondence Outlets:

Perceiving that youngsters put themselves out there in different ways, grown-ups ought to give an assortment of correspondence outlets. This might incorporate verbal correspondence, imaginative articulation, play, or other innovative exercises. Offering numerous roads for articulation permits youngsters to pick the mode that feels generally good for them.

Advance a Positive Climate:

A positive and steady climate cultivates solid turn of events and decreases the probability of misinterpretations. Making spaces where youngsters feel esteemed, regarded, and urged to put themselves out there adds to a good environment that supports their close to home prosperity.

Deciphering the Language of Experience growing up Conduct

Examining normal misinterpretations of kids' ways of behaving requires a nuanced comprehension of the multi-layered nature of young life articulation. As grown-ups explore the mind boggling scene of life as a youngster ways of behaving, they assume an essential part in forming conditions that cultivate solid turn of events, powerful correspondence, and steady connections.

Perceiving that kids convey through a different scope of ways of behaving permits grown-ups to move toward misinterpretations with interest, compassion, and a promise to grasping the exceptional viewpoints of every kid. By cultivating open correspondence, building confiding in connections, and looking for proficient direction when required, grownups add to establishing conditions where youngsters feel seen, heard, and comprehended.

Interpreting the language of experience growing up conduct is a continuous excursion that requires constant learning, versatility, and a profound appreciation for the uniqueness of every kid. As grown-ups participate in the specialty of understanding, they disentangle the layers of young life articulation, preparing for responsive providing care, positive turn of events, and the development of a steady local area for the future.

6.2 How cultural and generational gaps can contribute to misunderstandings.

Social and generational holes address rich woven artworks of variety, formed by particular encounters, viewpoints, and values. In any case, the convergences of these holes can at times prompt misconceptions, misinterpretations, and correspondence challenges.

This investigation digs into the diverse elements of social and generational contrasts, revealing the manners by which these holes add to misconceptions and offering experiences into cultivating multifaceted and intergenerational understanding.

Social Holes:

Social holes emerge from contrasts in values, convictions, customs, correspondence styles, and cultural standards among people from different social foundations. These holes can appear in different settings, like work environments, instructive settings, and relational connections, making difficulties in successful correspondence and common getting it.

Correspondence Styles:

Social contrasts significantly impact correspondence styles. In high-setting societies, correspondence depends vigorously on non-verbal signals, setting, and shared encounters, while low-setting societies focus on express verbal correspondence. At the point when people from these differentiating societies connect, errors might emerge due to varying assumptions about how data is conveyed and deciphered.

Accepted practices and Decorum:

Accepted practices and manners change broadly across societies, impacting ways of behaving, signals, and relational associations. What might be viewed as courteous or aware in one culture might be seen diversely in another. Misconceptions can happen when people know nothing about or misjudge these social subtleties, prompting accidental offense or disarray.

Values and Convictions:

Social qualities and convictions shape people's perspectives, impacting their needs, dynamic cycles, and moral contemplations. At the point when people from various social foundations participate in cooperative endeavors, clashes might emerge in the event that these basic qualities and convictions are not perceived or recognized. Connecting these holes requires a readiness to investigate and value different points of view.

Progressive system and Authority:

Shifting mentalities toward progressive system and authority add to social holes. In certain societies, a various leveled structure is esteemed, with clear differentiations between people in light of status or age. Interestingly, populist societies focus on equity and open correspondence. Errors can happen when people from progressive societies see populist approaches as impolite, while those from libertarian societies might see various leveled structures as unbending or smothering.

Time Direction:

Various mentalities toward time, like an emphasis on reliability or a more adaptable methodology, add to social holes.

In societies that focus on dependability, deferrals might be seen as impolite, while in societies with a more loosened up time direction, severe adherence to timetables might be viewed as excessively unbending. Spanning these holes includes perceiving and adjusting to assorted social viewpoints on time.

Generational Holes:

Generational holes come from contrasts in age, childhood, and cultural impacts. Every age conveys its own arrangement of values, assumptions, and correspondence styles, adding to unmistakable approaches to moving toward life and connections. Exploring generational contrasts is fundamental for cultivating coordinated effort and understanding across assorted age gatherings.

Innovation and Correspondence:

Mechanical progressions have formed the correspondence styles of various ages. More youthful ages, like Recent college grads and Age Z, frequently float towards computerized correspondence and virtual entertainment, while more seasoned ages might favor customary types of correspondence. Errors can emerge when suppositions are made about favored correspondence channels, prompting potential correspondence breakdowns.

Work environment Assumptions:

Every age carries extraordinary assumptions to the working environment in regards to administration styles, balance between fun and serious activities, and vocation movement. For instance, more seasoned ages might focus on steadfastness and strength, esteeming long haul responsibilities, while more youthful ages might look for adaptability, reason driven work, and fast professional success. Crossing over these holes requires making comprehensive working environment societies that oblige assorted generational assumptions.

Mentalities Toward Power:

Mentalities toward power and authority styles can fluctuate fundamentally across ages. Conservatives and Gen X-ers might esteem various leveled structures and legitimate authority, while more youthful ages might favor cooperative and comprehensive administration styles. Mistaken assumptions might emerge when assumptions around power and dynamic cycles are not adjusted, requiring open correspondence and adaptability.

Hard working attitude and Values:

Generational contrasts in hard working attitude and values can add to errors in proficient settings. For example, more seasoned ages might see more youthful specialists as less dedicated because of their craving for balance between fun and serious activities, while more youthful ages might see more seasoned partners as impervious to change. Recognizing and valuing different work styles and values can assist with spanning these generational holes.

Ways to deal with Change and Advancement:

Perspectives toward change and advancement frequently contrast among ages. More youthful ages might embrace change as a chance for development and improvement, while more seasoned ages might move toward it with mindfulness or inclination for security. Misconceptions can happen when the speed of progress isn't lined up with individual solace levels, underscoring the significance of cultivating a culture that values both practice and development.

Convergences of Social and Generational Holes:

The convergences of social and generational holes make a mind boggling scene where people explore different layers of variety. Understanding how these holes converge is vital for encouraging comprehensive conditions and moderating the potential for mistaken assumptions.

Language and Correspondence Subtleties:

The convergence of social and generational holes can appear in language and correspondence subtleties. Contrasts in language capability, articulations, and correspondence styles might emerge from both social and generational impacts. People should be receptive to these subtleties to stay away from misinterpretations and cultivate compelling cross-generational and diverse correspondence.

Ways to deal with Variety and Consideration:

Social and generational holes can impact people's ways to deal with variety and consideration. More youthful ages might put a more grounded accentuation on social responsiveness, value, and civil rights, while more seasoned ages might have alternate points of view on these issues. Connecting these holes includes encouraging a common obligation to inclusivity while regarding different points of view on the significance and techniques for accomplishing it.

Mentalities Toward Change and Custom:

The crossing point of social and generational holes frequently assumes a critical part in mentalities toward change and custom. Societies that esteem custom might conflict with generational inclinations for development. Effectively exploring these convergences requires perceiving the innate pressure and figuring out some shared interest that regards both social legacy and the requirement for transformation.

Work environment Elements and Orders:

Social and generational holes can affect work environment elements, especially as far as orders and correspondence structures. Societies with solid various leveled customs might line up with more seasoned ages' inclinations for organized power, while more youthful ages might look for additional cooperative and level authoritative designs. Tending to these holes includes establishing adaptable working environment conditions that oblige assorted social and generational assumptions.

Instructive Methodologies:

Instructive settings are another field where social and generational holes converge. Different social assumptions about schooling might adjust or conflict with generational inclinations for learning styles and approaches. Understanding and valuing these convergences are essential for instructors and foundations trying to establish comprehensive learning conditions.

Systems for Spanning Holes and Cultivating Understanding:

Exploring the mind boggling territory of social and generational holes requires deliberate endeavors to encourage figuring out, correspondence, and joint effort. A few procedures can add to crossing over these holes and establishing conditions that celebrate variety:

Social Skill Preparing:

Furnishing social ability preparing outfits people with the information and abilities expected to really explore social contrasts. Such preparation incorporates understanding social subtleties, correspondence styles, and tending to possible inclinations. Integrating generational mindfulness into these projects improves members' capacity to explore the crossing points of social and generational variety.

Open Discourse and Correspondence:

Empowering open discourse is fundamental for crossing over holes and encouraging comprehension. Making spaces for people to share their points of view, encounters, and assumptions works with correspondence across social and generational lines. Open correspondence dissipates generalizations, right misinterpretations, and construct shared regard.

Mentorship and Opposite Mentorship Projects:

Mentorship programs that pair people from various ages and social foundations give amazing open doors to shared learning. Turn around mentorship, where more youthful people guide more seasoned partners, can be especially viable in sharing bits of knowledge into contemporary issues, innovation, and changing cultural elements.

Comprehensive Arrangements and Practices:

Laying out comprehensive arrangements and practices in working environments and instructive organizations is critical for obliging different social and generational necessities. Adaptability in work plans, acknowledgment of social occasions, and comprehensive dynamic cycles add to establishing conditions where people feel esteemed and comprehended.

Social Trades and Festivities:

Sorting out social trades and festivities gives valuable open doors to people to find out about and value each other's societies and customs. These occasions make a feeling of shared festival and advance a more profound comprehension of the rich variety present locally.

Variety and Consideration Advisory groups:

Laying out variety and consideration panels can act as a committed space for tending to social and generational holes. These councils can make progress toward making strategies, coordinating mindfulness programs, and executing drives that advance inclusivity and understanding.

Adaptability in Correspondence Styles:

Perceiving and obliging different correspondence styles is fundamental for compelling culturally diverse and cross-generational correspondence. Stressing clearness in correspondence, giving open doors to both composed and verbal articulation, and making spaces for undivided attention add to a climate where people can impart serenely.

Social and Generational Responsiveness Preparing:

Notwithstanding broad social ability preparing, explicit responsiveness preparing that tends to the convergences of social and generational variety can upgrade mindfulness. This preparing can investigate the one of a kind difficulties and potential open doors introduced by the interchange of social and generational variables.

Developing Compassion:

Developing compassion includes effectively trying to comprehend and value the encounters and points of view of others. This incorporates perceiving the effect of social and generational impacts on individual ways of behaving, choices, and values. Sympathy shapes the establishment for building significant associations and crossing over holes.

Local area Commitment and Joint effort:

Drawing in with different networks and encouraging joint effort across social and generational lines reinforces social bonds and advances understanding. Cooperative people group projects, social celebrations, and intergenerational exercises set out open doors for shared encounters and learning.

6.3 Bridging the communication divide between parents and children.

Correspondence shapes the bedrock of connections, and no place is this more basic than in the parent-youngster dynamic. Nonetheless, the generational and experiential contrasts among guardians and youngsters frequently make a correspondence partition that can prompt errors, disappointment, and stressed connections. This investigation digs into the multi-layered nature of parent-youngster correspondence, revealing insight into the difficulties that add to the separation and offering techniques to cultivate significant associations.

Understanding the Correspondence Separation:

The correspondence split among guardians and kids is a nuanced interaction of generational differences, developing cultural standards, and individual encounters. These variables add to different correspondence styles, assumptions, and points of view, making obstacles in compelling exchange.

Generational Contrasts:

The consistently advancing scene of cultural standards and values shapes generational contrasts in correspondence. Guardians frequently bring correspondence styles established in their childhood, affected by social standards and encounters. Kids, then again, explore a quickly impacting world with unmistakable correspondence modes, impacted by innovation, peer collaborations, and developing social patterns.

Innovation's Effect:

The appearance of innovation has changed correspondence however has likewise presented a critical hole between ages. Guardians might find it trying to adjust to the fast speed of mechanical headways, while youngsters easily explore advanced stages and virtual entertainment. This innovative dissimilarity can impede successful correspondence, making it significant to overcome this issue for significant association.

Moving Cultural Standards:

Cultural standards go through steady change, affecting correspondence assumptions among guardians and youngsters. Changes in perspectives toward freedom, individual articulation, and dynamic independence can make pressure when guardians and youngsters hold contrasting perspectives on these cultural changes. Exploring these moving standards requires open exchange and common comprehension.

Parental Power versus Autonomy:

The customary job of guardians as power figures might conflict with youngsters' developing requirement for freedom and self-articulation. Finding some kind of harmony between keeping up with parental power and encouraging youngsters' independence is a fragile errand. Errors might emerge when assumptions around power and autonomy are not conveyed and haggled successfully.

Social Impacts:

Social impacts assume a urgent part in forming correspondence styles inside families. Outsider families, for example, may wrestle with the conflict between conventional social qualities and the social digestion of more youthful ages. The exchange of these social elements adds one more layer to the correspondence partition, requiring awareness and social ability.

Systems for Spanning the Correspondence Gap:

Crossing over the correspondence split among guardians and youngsters includes deliberate endeavors to see each other's points of view, adjust to developing correspondence styles, and encourage a climate of trust and receptiveness. A few methodologies can add to limiting this hole and sustaining better correspondence channels.

Undivided attention:

Undivided attention frames the groundwork of successful correspondence. The two guardians and kids benefit from really paying attention to one another's contemplations, concerns, and sentiments. This includes really focusing, staying away from interferences, and looking for explanation to guarantee an extensive comprehension of one another's viewpoints.

Sympathy as an Extension:

Developing sympathy is vital for spanning the correspondence partition. Guardians ought to endeavor to comprehend the special difficulties and tensions looked by their youngsters, while kids ought to relate to the encounters and worries of their folks. Perceiving the feelings fundamental correspondence advances a more profound association.

Open and Non-Critical Exchange:

Laying out open and non-critical correspondence channels makes a place of refuge for the two guardians and kids to uninhibitedly articulate their thoughts. Saving assumptions, staying away from fault, and cultivating a climate where sentiments are regarded add to more productive and open exchange.

Figuring out Generational Viewpoints:

The two guardians and kids can profit according to figuring out generational viewpoints. Guardians ought to recognize the unmistakable difficulties and impacts forming the universe of their youngsters, while kids ought to see the value in the encounters and astuteness their folks offer that would be useful. This common comprehension prepares for connecting generational holes in correspondence.

Adjusting to Mechanical Changes:

Recognizing and adjusting to mechanical changes is urgent for compelling correspondence in the computerized age. Guardians can find proactive ways to really get to know computerized stages, web-based entertainment, and specialized instruments usually utilized by their kids. This transformation shows a readiness to take part in their kids' reality and works with smoother correspondence.

Laying out Shared view:

Recognizing divided interests and laying out shared belief encourages more grounded associations among guardians and kids.

Whether through shared exercises, side interests, or common objectives, finding shared traits makes an establishment for significant correspondence. This common ground helps span holes and supports that in spite of contrasts, there are areas of association.

Developing Ability to understand individuals on a deeper level:

The two guardians and kids can profit from developing capacity to understand people on a deeper level. This includes perceiving and grasping one's own feelings and those of others. Guardians can direct their kids in creating the ability to appreciate anyone on a deeper level, while likewise displaying these abilities in their own correspondence. The capacity to understand individuals on a profound level upgrades the capacity to explore complex sentiments and advances better collaborations.

Setting Clear Assumptions:

Clear correspondence includes setting assumptions about obligations, limits, and social standards. Guardians ought to convey their assumptions straightforwardly, permitting youngsters to grasp the reasoning behind rules and rules. Essentially, kids ought to communicate their necessities and assumptions, cultivating a cooperative way to deal with relational peculiarities.

Family Gatherings:

Laying out ordinary family gatherings gives an assigned space to open correspondence. These gatherings can include conversations about forthcoming occasions, concerns, or choices that influence the family. Empowering cooperation from all relatives encourages a feeling of inclusivity and fortifies the nuclear family.

Parental Direction versus Strong Direction:

Moving from a simply definitive position to a more strong and direction situated approach can improve correspondence. Guardians can be guides and tutors, offering backing and exhortation without forcing choices.

This approach encourages trust and permits kids to feel appreciated and regarded.

Empowering Individual Articulation:

Perceiving and celebrating individual articulation is fundamental for connecting the correspondence hole. Guardians ought to urge their kids to communicate their remarkable personalities, sentiments, and yearnings. Establishing a climate where singularity is esteemed supports a feeling of acknowledgment and receptiveness.

Social Responsiveness and Ability:

For families with different social foundations, social responsiveness and skill are vital. The two guardians and youngsters ought to endeavor to comprehend and value each other's social viewpoints. Participating in discussions about social qualities, customs, and assumptions helps assemble spans across social contrasts.

Defeating Explicit Correspondence Difficulties:

Tending to explicit correspondence challenges requires custom fitted procedures that recognize the special idea of each issue. Here are some normal correspondence challenges inside parent-kid connections and ways of defeating them:

Tending to Struggle:

Struggle is unavoidable in any relationship, yet the way things are taken care of is essential. Open correspondence during seasons of contention includes communicating sentiments tranquilly, effectively paying attention to one another's points of view, and working cooperatively toward goals. Looking for compromises and settling on something worth agreeing on explores clashes helpfully.

Exploring Puberty:

Puberty is a stage set apart by tremendous changes, both physical and close to home. Guardians ought to move toward this stage with persistence, compassion, and a comprehension of the difficulties looked by their kids. Establishing a strong climate where young people feel happy with communicating their thoughts reinforces the parent-kid security.

Managing Insider facts and Protection:

Adjusting the requirement for protection with parental concern requires a fragile methodology. Guardians ought to convey the significance of genuineness while regarding their youngsters' requirement for individual space. Laying out trust through open correspondence decreases the probability of mysteries and urges youngsters to trust in their folks.

Taking care of Scholastic Tensions:

Scholastic tensions can strain parent-kid correspondence, particularly when assumptions vary. Guardians ought to keep up with practical assumptions, accentuating exertion over results. Empowering open correspondence about scholastic difficulties, offering help, and working together on systems for progress cultivate a positive scholarly climate.

Overseeing Innovation Use:

Directing innovation use inside the family requires clear correspondence and laid out rules. Guardians ought to include their kids in conversations about mindful innovation use, tending to worries, and defining settled upon limits. Cooperative direction advances a common perspective of the family's way to deal with innovation.

Progressing to Autonomy:

The progress to autonomy can be trying for the two guardians and youngsters. Clear correspondence about assumptions, obligations, and the progressive shift toward independence explores this change without a hitch. Guardians ought to give direction while permitting space to their youngsters to foster freedom and thinking abilities.

Chapter 7

Rediscovering Connection

In the consistently developing scene of the advanced age, portrayed by the ubiquity of screens, web-based entertainment, and moment correspondence, the idea of association has taken on new aspects. While innovation has brought individuals closer across immense distances, it has likewise presented difficulties that can prevent significant associations in our regular routines. This investigation dives into the complexities of rediscovering association in the computerized age, looking at the effect of innovation on connections and offering bits of knowledge into cultivating legitimate associations in a world overwhelmed by screens.

The Computerized Scene:

The computerized age has reformed the manner in which we associate, convey, and connect with each other. With the multiplication of cell phones, online entertainment stages, and virtual specialized instruments, our communications are progressively interceded by screens. While these innovations offer uncommon open doors for worldwide association, they additionally present difficulties to the profundity and validness of our connections.

Virtual Availability versus Profound Closeness:

The virtual network worked with by advanced stages frequently misses the mark in developing close to home closeness.

While we can share minutes, updates, and messages immediately, the profundity of profound association might be compromised. The promptness of advanced correspondence once in a while focuses on quickness over profundity, leaving nuanced feelings and nuances lost in the computerized interpretation.

Measuring Connections:

Virtual entertainment, with its measurements of preferences, remarks, and supporters, has acquainted a quantifiable perspective with connections. The quantity of internet based communications can turn into a proportion of social approval, possibly eclipsing the subjective parts of veritable association. Chasing advanced insistence, people might wind up exploring the fragile harmony among validness and the longing for social endorsement.

Computerized Weariness and Burnout:

The steady flood of advanced data and the requests of virtual availability add to computerized weariness and burnout. The strain to remain continually associated, answer speedily to messages, and keep a web-based presence can negatively affect mental and close to home prosperity. In the journey for association, people might end up wrestling with the unseen side-effects of advanced exhaustion.

Difficulties to Association in the Advanced Age:

While advanced devices have irrefutably worked with worldwide correspondence, they have additionally presented difficulties that influence the nature of our associations. Understanding these difficulties is fundamental in exploring the computerized scene with purposefulness and cultivating certifiable associations.

Shallow Commitment:

The quickness and promptness of computerized correspondence can cultivate shallow commitment. Fast messages, emoticons, and brief remarks might come up short on profundity and extravagance of up close and personal communications. The test lies in rising above the impediments of virtual correspondence to support significant associations that go past the surface.

Relative Social Elements:

Online entertainment stages frequently become fields for near friendly elements, where people analyze their lives, accomplishments, and encounters with those of others. This relative viewpoint can prompt insecurities, envy, or the steady quest for outside approval. Valid association might be obstructed as people curate their web-based personas to fit cultural assumptions.

Advanced Interruptions:

The pervasiveness of screens and advanced gadgets can make interruptions that obstruct certifiable association.

In eye to eye communications, the draw of notices, messages, and the appeal of consistent web-based commitment might redirect consideration and impede the nature of commitment. Being genuinely present yet intellectually somewhere else represents a test to cultivating genuine association.

Online Disinhibition Impact:

The web-based disinhibition impact, where people feel freed from accepted practices and restraints in virtual spaces, can affect the validness of computerized communications. Online namelessness or saw distance can prompt way of behaving that varies from genuine cooperations, possibly preventing the foundation of real associations in view of trust and legitimacy.

Methodologies for Rediscovering Association:

In the midst of the difficulties introduced by the computerized age, deliberate systems can be utilized to rediscover and reinforce valid associations. These techniques envelop careful innovation use, focusing on significant cooperations, and developing a harmony between the virtual and the genuine.

Careful Innovation Use:

Embracing careful innovation use includes being deliberate about how, when, and why we draw in with advanced gadgets. Laying out limits for screen time, particularly during eye to eye cooperations, permits people to be completely present at the time. By deliberately picking when to draw in with innovation, people can lessen computerized interruptions and upgrade the nature of their associations.

Adjusting Virtual and Eye to eye Associations:

Finding some kind of harmony among virtual and eye to eye associations is fundamental for developing true associations. While computerized stages offer helpful ways of remaining associated, concentrating profoundly on face to face gatherings, get-togethers, and shared encounters encourages a more profound feeling of association. Adjusting the virtual and the genuine guarantees that connections are advanced through different methods of association.

Embracing Weakness:

Credible associations flourish with weakness — the eagerness to share one's actual self, including instabilities, fears, and yearnings. In the computerized domain, embracing weakness can include moving past organized web-based personas and sharing certifiable encounters. Opening up to other people, even in virtual spaces, fabricates trust and cultivates a feeling of association that rises above superficial communications.

Better standards without compromise in Advanced Collaborations:

Focusing on better standards without compromise in advanced collaborations includes moving past shallow commitment.

Rather than zeroing in exclusively on the quantity of web-based connections, people can make progress toward additional significant and considerable discussions. This shift stresses the profundity of association as opposed to the sheer volume of online commitment.

Advanced Detox and Turning off:

Perceiving the requirement for intermittent computerized detoxes and it is imperative to turn off from consistent network. Planned parts from computerized gadgets permit people to recalibrate, diminish advanced weariness, and reconnect with the current second. Turning off, even momentarily, advances care and improves the nature of resulting connections.

Developing Advanced Compassion:

Developing advanced compassion includes perceiving the human behind the screen and understanding the feelings passed on through computerized correspondence. This compassion reaches out to thinking about the effect of online communications on others and being aware of the likely confusion of messages. Advanced sympathy upgrades the nature of virtual associations and advances figuring out in the computerized domain.

Defining Correspondence Limits:

Laying out clear correspondence limits guarantees that people have the space to adjust their virtual and genuine collaborations. Imparting inclinations with respect to reaction times, online accessibility, and the idea of computerized correspondence oversees assumptions and decreases the strain for consistent network.

Making Shared Computerized Spaces:

Cultivating association in the computerized age can include making shared advanced spaces that work with significant connections. This could incorporate internet based networks, bunch talks revolved around shared interests, or cooperative advanced projects. These common spaces give roads to more profound associations past the requirements of individual profiles and timetables.

Advancing Computerized Presence with Aim:

Purposeful advanced presence includes careful sharing and commitment on the web. Rather than capitulating to the tension of consistent updates, people can zero in on sharing significant substance and effectively taking part in conversations that line up with their qualities. This deliberate methodology adds to a more credible web-based presence.

Empowering Advanced Limits in Connections:

Inside private connections, defining shared computerized limits guarantees that the two players feel regarded and heard. This might include examining inclinations for sharing individual data web based, regarding each other's security, and mutually settling fair and square of advanced commitment that upgrades instead of blocks the relationship.

Developing Advanced Care:

Developing advanced care is an all-encompassing methodology that envelops mindfulness, deliberateness, and cognizant decisions in the computerized domain. Computerized care includes being available in advanced cooperations, figuring out the effect of online ways of behaving, and settling on decisions that line up with one's qualities and the objective of cultivating real associations.

Considering Advanced Ways of behaving:

Considering advanced ways of behaving includes intermittent self-evaluation of one's internet based communications. People can ask themselves inquiries, for example, "How would I feel in the wake of investing energy in virtual entertainment?" or "Is my web-based commitment lined up with my qualities?" This intelligent practice upgrades mindfulness and illuminates purposeful decisions in the computerized space.

Rehearsing Advanced Holidays:

Advanced holidays, or purposeful breaks from computerized commitment, give amazing open doors to reflection and revival. Whether it's daily, an end of the week, or a more broadened period, rehearsing computerized vacations permits people to recalibrate their relationship with innovation, decrease advanced exhaustion, and rediscover the worth of non-computerized encounters.

Building Advanced Customs:

Incorporating advanced customs includes integrating purposeful practices into everyday schedules. This could incorporate saving committed time for eye to eye discussions, laying out gadget free zones in the home, or making customs that mark the change from computerized commitment to disconnected minutes. These customs add to a careful and adjusted way to deal with innovation use.

Encouraging Advanced Associations with Reason:

Encouraging advanced associations with reason includes looking for significant connections on the web. Rather than carelessly looking at takes care of, people can effectively draw in with content that lines up with their inclinations, values, and objectives. Deliberate computerized commitment adds to a feeling of satisfaction and association in the virtual space.

Teaching on Advanced Prosperity:

Instruction on advanced prosperity is urgent for people, all things considered. Showing computerized education, moral web-based conduct, and the effect of innovation on emotional wellness outfits people with the information to capably explore the advanced scene. Training encourages an aggregate comprehension of the significance of equilibrium and prosperity in the computerized age.

7.1 Strategies for rebuilding and strengthening the parent-child relationship.

Methodologies for Revamping and Reinforcing the Parent-Kid Relationship

The parent-youngster relationship is a foundation of self-improvement, giving the establishment to close to home prosperity, confidence, and social collaborations. Notwithstanding, difficulties might emerge that strain this essential bond. Whether impacted by life changes, correspondence breakdowns, or outside factors, the requirement for revamping and reinforcing the parent-kid relationship is entirely expected. This investigation dives into procedures pointed toward rejuvenating and sustaining a sound, tough association among guardians and youngsters.

Grasping the Elements:

Prior to diving into procedures, it's crucial for handle the basic elements that can add to a stressed parent-youngster relationship. Different elements might assume a part, including:

Correspondence Breakdown:

Ineffectual correspondence or an absence of open discourse can prompt misconceptions, disappointment, and a feeling of profound distance among guardians and youngsters.

Life Changes:

Life advances, like separation, movement, or changes in relational intricacies, can disturb the balance of the parent-kid relationship. Acclimating to these progressions might require purposeful endeavors to modify associations.

Nurturing Styles:

Disparate nurturing styles can make clashes in assumptions, discipline, and navigation. Fitting these styles is essential for cultivating a firm and steady family climate.

Outer Impacts:

Outer impacts, for example, peer pressure, cultural assumptions, or scholarly pressure, can influence a kid's way of behaving and correspondence with guardians. Understanding these impacts is imperative in resolving fundamental issues.

Profound Strength:

The two guardians and youngsters might confront difficulties that influence their profound versatility. Reinforcing close to home prosperity is fundamental for reconstructing a versatile parent-kid relationship.

Systems for Remaking and Reinforcing:

Transparent Correspondence:

Cultivating transparent correspondence is the bedrock of a sound parent-kid relationship. Making a place of refuge for discourse, where the two players feel appreciated and comprehended, is critical. Empowering youngsters to communicate their sentiments and contemplations

unafraid of judgment constructs trust and fortifies the profound association.

Undivided attention:

Undivided attention is a useful asset for building understanding and
association. Guardians ought to put forth a cognizant attempt to listen
mindfully to their kids' interests, approving their feelings and exhibiting
sympathy. This complementary act of undivided attention develops a
feeling of common regard.

Quality Time:

Quality time spent together is instrumental in revamping and reinforcing the parent-youngster relationship. Participating in shared exercises,
leisure activities, or basically having committed one-on-one time encourages bonds and makes positive recollections. This deliberate interest in
one another's lives adds to a feeling of association.

Communicating Fondness:

Showing friendship through words, motions, and actual touch is a
strong method for supporting the profound bond. Verbal articulations of
affection, embraces, and insistences give consolation and add to a positive profound environment inside the family.

Setting Reasonable Assumptions:

Setting reasonable assumptions for the two guardians and youngsters
is critical. Ridiculous assumptions can prompt disillusionment and disappointment. Recognizing and valuing each other's assets and limits
cultivates a steady climate and oversees assumptions.

Family Customs and Customs:

Laying out family customs and customs makes a feeling of progres-
sion and shared personality. Whether it's a week by week family supper,
occasion customs, or unique trips, these ceremonies give open doors to
association, cultivating a feeling of having a place and solidarity.

Compassion and Understanding:

Developing compassion includes seeing each other's points of view and
feelings. The two guardians and kids benefit from recognizing and valuing
the special difficulties they face. This common perspective structures the
reason for empathy and reinforces the profound bond.

Compromise Abilities:

Struggle is unavoidable in any relationship, however having successful
compromise abilities is essential.

Showing youngsters and guardians how to communicate their requirements, listen effectively, and find commonly pleasant arrangements adds
to a better unique. Settling clashes usefully builds up the strength of the
relationship.

Nurturing Studios and Guiding:

Looking for outer help, for example, nurturing studios or advising, can give significant experiences and instruments to modifying the parent-youngster relationship. Proficient direction offers systems customized to the particular difficulties looked by the family, working with useful correspondence and association.

Strength Building:

Building strength, both in guardians and youngsters, is fundamental for exploring life's difficulties. Empowering versatility, adapting abilities, and a positive outlook adds to close to home strength and improves the family's capacity to climate hardships together.

Shared Independent direction:

Including kids in age-proper dynamic cycles enables them and cultivates a feeling of independence. Cooperative independent direction, where guardians and kids talk about and settle on specific viewpoints together, reinforces the feeling of organization inside the family.

Demonstrating Solid Connections:

Guardians act as essential good examples for their kids. Displaying solid connections, viable correspondence, and critical thinking sets a positive model. Youngsters gain important examples from seeing how their folks explore difficulties and support positive associations.

Individual and Family Objectives:

Laying out individual and family objectives gives a feeling of motivation and heading. Cooperating towards normal targets cultivates a common vision and builds up the possibility that every relative assumes a urgent part in the aggregate achievement and prosperity of the family.

Observe Accomplishments:

Praising accomplishments, whether enormous or little, makes a culture of affirmation and inspiration. Perceiving each other's achievements encourages a strong climate where everybody feels esteemed and appreciated.

Careful Nurturing:

Rehearsing careful nurturing includes being completely present at the time, without judgment. Careful nurturing supports attention to one's viewpoints and responses, encouraging deliberate and merciful reactions to the requirements of youngsters. This careful methodology adds to a more adjusted and associated parent-youngster relationship.

Saying 'sorry' and Excusing:

Recognizing missteps and offering certifiable statements of regret when vital is a strong signal. Similarly, showing youngsters the worth of pardoning and exhibiting the ability to excuse cultivates a culture of close to home versatility and common comprehension.

Energize Uniqueness:

Perceiving and commending every relative's uniqueness is vital. Empowering youngsters to investigate their inclinations, express their extraordinary characters, and seek after their interests supports that variety inside the family isn't just acknowledged however celebrated.

Advanced Equilibrium:

In the period of computerized network, keeping a good overall arrangement between screen time and eye to eye communications is fundamental. Laying out limits around innovation use advances more significant associations inside the family.

Appreciation Practices:

Developing appreciation rehearses inside the family empowers a positive outlook. Offering thanks for one another and the common encounters builds up the appreciation for the familial bond.

Predictable Support:

Building and fortifying the parent-youngster relationship is a continuous interaction that requires steady support. Incorporating these procedures into day to day existence and schedules guarantees that the relational intricacy is consistently supported and stays strong.

7.2 The power of active listening and open communication.

Correspondence is the backbone of connections, and inside the unpredictable texture of human associations, undivided attention and open correspondence arise as strong impetuses for grasping, sympathy, and common development. This investigation digs into the significant effect of undivided attention and open correspondence on encouraging further associations in different circles of life.

Undivided attention: The Specialty of Presence

Undivided attention is something other than hearing words; it is the craft of being completely present at the time, sensitive to the speaker's words, feelings, and non-verbal signals. With regards to connections, particularly inside the parent-kid dynamic, undivided attention fills in as a foundation for building trust, encouraging comprehension, and establishing a supporting climate.

Making a Place of refuge:

Undivided attention makes a safe and non-critical space where people feel appreciated and esteemed.

In the parent-youngster relationship, giving this safe climate permits kids to offer their viewpoints, fears, and goals unafraid of analysis, empowering receptiveness and close to home association.

Figuring out Indeed:

Words are nevertheless one layer of correspondence; undivided attention digs further to grasp the implicit feelings and subtleties behind the words. This degree of understanding is especially urgent in connections where unexpressed sentiments can hold onto and putrefy. Guardians who effectively stand by listening to their youngsters can get a handle on the express message as well as the basic feelings, encouraging a more significant association.

Approval and Compassion:

Through undivided attention, people impart approval and sympathy. The demonstration of recognizing and approving somebody's sentiments, regardless of whether they vary from one's own, is an intense confirmation of their close to home insight. In the parent-youngster relationship, this approval fabricates a kid's close to home strength and a feeling of being figured out, establishing the groundwork for a solid bond.

Upgrading Relationship Quality:

The nature of a relationship is straightforwardly connected to the profundity of understanding between people. Undivided attention upgrades relationship quality by guaranteeing that the two players feel seen and heard. In the parent-youngster relationship, this profundity of association advances a feeling of trust and close to home security that is fundamental for a kid's solid turn of events.

Open Correspondence: Supporting Straightforward Exchanges

Open correspondence remains inseparable with undivided attention, making a harmonious relationship that frames the reason for straightforward discoursed. Whether in private connections, proficient settings, or inside networks, open correspondence is the doorway to shared regard, critical thinking, and cooperative development.

Cultivating Trust:

Trust is the bedrock of any significant relationship, and open correspondence is the way to building and keeping up with that trust. At the point when people go ahead and offer their viewpoints, concerns, and yearnings unafraid of judgment or retaliation, an underpinning of trust is cemented. In families, trust frames the paste that ties guardians and kids together in a strong and sustaining bond.

Critical thinking and Compromise:

Open correspondence is instrumental in exploring difficulties and clashes. In any relationship, conflicts are unavoidable, yet how they are tended to characterizes the soundness of the association.

Through open correspondence, people can take part in helpful discoursed, seeing each other's viewpoints, and cooperatively tracking down arrangements. In the parent-kid relationship, this ability prepares families to explore the intricacies of development and advancement.

Empowering Individual Articulation:

Open correspondence supports individual articulation, establishing a climate where each voice is esteemed. In families, permitting youngsters to offer their viewpoints and thoughts cultivates a feeling of independence and self-esteem. This consolation of individual articulation lays the preparation for kids to foster areas of strength for an of character and fearlessness.

Developing Ability to appreciate anyone on a deeper level:

The ability to appreciate individuals on a deeper level is supported through open correspondence that energizes the investigation and comprehension of feelings. In families, talking about feelings transparently assists kids with creating the ability to understand anyone at their core, empowering them to explore complex sentiments and relational elements. This expertise is priceless in cultivating flexibility and building significant associations over the course of life.

Versatility and Adaptability:

Open correspondence advances versatility and adaptability inside connections. Life is dynamic, and the capacity to convey straightforwardly permits people to explore changes, advances, and unforeseen difficulties. In the parent-kid relationship, open correspondence assists families with adjusting to developing necessities and guarantees that the two guardians and youngsters feel upheld during seasons of progress.

Setting Assumptions:

Clear correspondence is fundamental for setting and overseeing assumptions. Whether in familial, expert, or group environments, conveying assumptions guarantees that all gatherings included are in total agreement. In families, setting assumptions transparently permits guardians and kids to grasp their jobs, obligations, and the aggregate vision for the nuclear family.

Building a Culture of Straightforwardness:

Open correspondence adds to the making of a culture of straightforwardness inside connections. At the point when people go ahead and share their considerations, encounters, and concerns straightforwardly, a feeling of solidarity and common perspective is developed. In families, this straightforwardness is central for building areas of strength for a versatile emotionally supportive network.

Advancing a Development Mentality:

A development mentality flourishes in a climate of open correspondence. At the point when people are urged to share their objectives, goals, and difficulties transparently, it cultivates a culture of consistent learning and improvement. In families, advancing a development outlook permits guardians and kids to help each other's private and aggregate turn of events.

The Collaboration of Undivided attention and Open Correspondence:

The genuine force of undivided attention and open correspondence lies in their collaboration. At the point when people effectively pay attention to one another, making a space of receptivity and understanding, open correspondence normally prospers. This proportional relationship upgrades the profundity of associations, whether between accomplices, partners, companions, or guardians and youngsters.

Developing Common Regard:

The collaboration of undivided attention and open correspondence develops common regard inside connections. At the point when people feel appreciated and esteemed, and when their contemplations and viewpoints are recognized through open correspondence, an underpinning of shared regard is laid out. In the parent-youngster relationship, this regard is basic for supporting a kid's identity worth and pride.

Fortifying Close to home Bonds:

The close to home securities produced through undivided attention and open correspondence are significant. At the point when people experience the bona fide association that comes from being really heard and perceived, close to home bonds are reinforced. In families, this profundity of association advances a feeling of having a place, love, and shared encounters that persevere through everyday hardship.

Struggle Change:

The cooperative energy of these relational abilities changes clashes from antagonistic difficulties into valuable open doors for development and understanding. At the point when clashes are drawn closer with undivided attention and open correspondence, the center movements from fault and preventiveness to cooperative critical thinking. In the parent-youngster relationship, this change constructs versatility and braces the connection between ages.

Working with Shared Objectives:

Undivided attention and open correspondence add to the arrangement of shared objectives inside connections. At the point when people are receptive to one another's desires and concerns, cooperative objective setting turns into a characteristic movement. In families, this arrangement guarantees that guardians and kids cooperate towards a typical vision for their aggregate prosperity and achievement.

Advancing Psychological wellness and Prosperity:

The comprehensive effect of undivided attention and open correspondence stretches out to psychological well-being and prosperity. At the point when people can communicate their feelings straightforwardly, get grasping through undivided attention, and take part in straightforward exchanges, the in general emotional wellness of the relationship is emphatically impacted. In families, this advances a sincerely sustaining climate that upholds the development and prospering of every relative.

Difficulties and Methodologies for Execution:

While the advantages of undivided attention and open correspondence are clear, carrying out these practices can present difficulties, particularly in the high speed, carefully determined world. Here are a few procedures for defeating these difficulties:

Time Responsibility:

The speedy idea of present day life can make carving out opportunity for undivided attention and open correspondence testing. Techniques incorporate booking committed family time, establishing a correspondence accommodating climate at home, and utilizing innovation carefully to work with associations.

Advanced Interruptions:

Innovation can be a two sided deal, both working with and blocking correspondence. Executing advanced detox periods, laying out innovation free zones inside the home, and defining limits for gadget use during family time can relieve the effect of computerized interruptions.

Generational Holes:

Various ages might move toward correspondence in an unexpected way. Spanning generational holes includes shared grasping, persistence, and an eagerness to adjust correspondence styles. Empowering intergenerational exchanges and esteeming assorted viewpoints add to successful correspondence across ages.

Social Varieties:

Social contrasts can impact correspondence standards and assumptions. Recognizing and regarding social varieties inside families, work environments, or networks is fundamental. Empowering open conversations about social contrasts cultivates understanding and inclusivity.

Building Relational abilities:

Creating solid relational abilities is a continuous interaction. Families, associations, and networks can put resources into studios, preparing projects, or assets that upgrade relational abilities. Instruction on the significance of undivided attention and open correspondence makes mindfulness and empowers constant improvement.

7.3 Embracing a more empathetic and attuned approach to parenting.

Nurturing is a perplexing dance of direction, backing, and understanding, where the elements among guardians and youngsters shape the establishment for a kid's personal prosperity and development. As of late, there has been a change in perspective in nurturing ways of thinking, with a developing acknowledgment of the significance of compassion and attunement in supporting sound parent-youngster connections. This investigation digs into the groundbreaking force of embracing a more sympathetic and adjusted way to deal with nurturing and the significant effect it has on cultivating association and close to home prosperity in kids.

Understanding Compassion in Nurturing:

Sympathy is the capacity to comprehend and discuss the thoughts of another. With regards to nurturing, sympathy includes venturing into the profound universe of a kid, perceiving their sentiments, and answering with understanding and empathy. This compassionate methodology lays the basis for a protected connection among guardians and kids, establishing a strong climate where youngsters feel seen, heard, and esteemed.

Perceiving and Approving Feelings:

Sympathetic nurturing starts with the major demonstration of perceiving and approving a kid's feelings. Whether it's satisfaction, pity, disappointment, or energy, recognizing and tolerating these feelings without judgment cultivates a feeling of close to home security. This acknowledgment imparts to the youngster that their sentiments are substantial and deserving of affirmation.

Making a Safe Profound Space:

A sympathetic methodology makes a safe close to home space where kids feel happy with communicating their feelings straightforwardly. This profound security is fundamental for youngsters to explore the intricacies of their sentiments and foster capacity to understand individuals on a deeper level. A protected close to home space empowers open correspondence and a confiding in parent-kid relationship.

Showing Close to home Guideline:

Sympathy stretches out to showing youngsters the expertise of close to home guideline. By displaying solid approaches to communicating and dealing with feelings, guardians furnish youngsters with fundamental instruments for exploring their own close to home scenes. This proactive methodology fabricates close to home flexibility as well as reinforces the parent-youngster bond.

Empowering Point of view Taking:

Sympathy includes point of view taking, grasping a circumstance according to one more's perspective.

In nurturing, empowering youngsters to consider others' points of view encourages compassion towards their companions, relatives, and the more extensive local area. This more extensive viewpoint develops sympathy and a feeling of interconnectedness.

Answering Requirements with Awareness:

A sympathetic parent answers a kid's necessities with responsiveness and attunement. This includes being receptive to the kid's signs, grasping their non-verbal signals, and answering instantly and properly. Aversion to a kid's requirements constructs an underpinning of trust, supporting the kid's conviction that all is good inside the parent-kid relationship.

Adjusted Nurturing: Tuning into the Youngster's Reality

Adjusted nurturing takes compassion to a more profound level, underscoring the significance of tuning into the youngster's reality on a significant close to home and mental level. It includes an elevated consciousness of the youngster's prompts, necessities, and remarkable character, making a responsive and strong nurturing style.

Perceiving Individual Contrasts:

Adjusted nurturing perceives and commends the singular distinctions among youngsters. Every kid is interesting, with their own disposition, assets, and difficulties. Adjusted guardians embrace and value these distinctions, fitting their way to deal with meet the particular requirements of every youngster.

Building Secure Connection:

Secure connection frames the bedrock of adjusted nurturing. It is portrayed by a kid's trust that their requirements will be met, and their feelings will be recognized. Adjusted guardians focus on building this protected connection by reliably answering a youngster's signals, making a feeling of safety and consistency.

Responsive Correspondence Styles:

Adjusted nurturing includes embracing responsive correspondence styles that line up with the youngster's formative stage. From early stages to immaturity, youngsters impart in differed ways. Adjusted guardians adjust their correspondence styles, guaranteeing that the kid feels comprehended and esteemed at each phase of their turn of events.

Careful Presence:

Careful presence is a center component of adjusted nurturing. It includes being completely present at the time with the youngster, liberated from interruptions and distractions. This careful presence conveys to the kid that they are vital, cultivating a profound feeling of association and significance.

Engaging the Youngster's Voice:

Adjusted guardians engage the youngster's voice by effectively uplifting and esteeming their perspectives and articulations. This strengthening imparts a feeling of independence and self-esteem in the youngster, adding to a solid improvement of character and fearlessness.

Influence on Close to home Prosperity:

The compassionate and adjusted way to deal with nurturing significantly affects a youngster's personal prosperity. Profound prosperity incorporates a kid's capacity to comprehend and deal with their feelings, structure good connections, and explore life's difficulties with versatility.

Close to home Versatility:

Kids raised with sympathy and attunement foster close to home versatility — the capacity to return from difficulties and mishaps. This versatility is sustained through the experience of being upheld and grasped in the midst of close to home misery, instructing kids that they can explore troubles fully backed up by their parental figures.

Positive Mental self portrait:

The sympathetic and adjusted nurturing style adds to the development of a positive mental self portrait in kids. At the point when kids feel perceived the truth about and esteemed, they incorporate a feeling of value and foster a good perspective on themselves. This positive mental self portrait turns into the establishment for solid confidence.

Laying out Solid Connections:

Youngsters who experience compassion and attunement in their early stages are bound to shape solid connections in adulthood. They get familiar with the significance of understanding and regarding others' feelings, encouraging good associations in light of compassion and common comprehension.

Compelling Survival techniques:

A compassionate and adjusted childhood furnishes kids with powerful survival methods. They figure out how to control their feelings, put themselves out there helpfully, and look for help when required. These adapting abilities are fundamental for exploring life's difficulties and keeping up with mental prosperity.

Improved Interactive abilities:

The capacity to relate be receptive to others upgrades a youngster's interactive abilities. Youngsters raised with these characteristics are bound to participate in prosocial conduct, team up actually with peers, and contribute decidedly to their social surroundings. These improved interactive abilities are significant resources in different life settings.

Difficulties and Procedures for Execution:

While the advantages of a sympathetic and adjusted way to deal with nurturing are apparent, there are difficulties to its execution in the present speedy and requesting world. Here are a few procedures for conquering these difficulties:

Using time productively:

The requests of present day life can make time usage a test for guardians. Procedures remember focusing on better standards when in doubt for collaborations, making committed family time, and consolidating careful practices to improve the nature of parent-kid connections.

Balance between serious and fun activities:
Adjusting work responsibilities with nurturing liabilities is a typical test. Methodologies include defining limits, laying out an encouraging group of people, and cultivating open correspondence with bosses about the significance of family time.

Social and Cultural Tensions:
Social and cultural assumptions can influence nurturing styles. Procedures incorporate perceiving and testing cultural standards that might subvert compassionate nurturing, looking for help from similar networks, and focusing on individualized approaches that line up with the kid's prosperity.

Advanced Interruptions:
The ubiquity of computerized gadgets represents a test to careful nurturing. Techniques incorporate carrying out innovation free zones and times, cultivating up close and personal connections, and demonstrating sound screen propensities for kids.

Parental Taking care of oneself:
Parental taking care of oneself is critical for keeping a compassionate and adjusted approach. Systems include focusing on taking care of oneself, looking for help from accomplices, family, or companions, and perceiving that parental prosperity straightforwardly influences the nature of collaborations with kids.

Molding a Merciful Future
Embracing a more sympathetic and adjusted way to deal with nurturing isn't simply a decision; it is an interest in the profound prosperity and fate of the future. The extraordinary force of sympathy goes past individual families — it swells through networks and adds to the production of a more empathetic and interconnected society.

As guardians develop sympathy and attunement in their nurturing venture, they add to a tradition of genuinely versatile, socially cognizant, and empathetic people. The effect is extensive, forming the manner in which people in the future methodology connections, explore difficulties, and contribute decidedly to the world.

In the embroidery of nurturing, the strings of compassion and attunement weave a story of figuring out, affection, and association. As we explore the intricacies of bringing kids up in the 21st 100 years, let us embrace the significant impact of a sympathetic and adjusted approach, perceiving that, in doing as such, we shape the close to home scene of our families as well as the humane texture of the world our youngsters will acquire.